St. Louis Cardinals 2020

A Baseball Companion

Edited by R.J. Anderson, Craig Goldstein and Bret Sayre

Baseball Prospectus

Craig Brown, Steven Goldman and David Pease, Consultant Editors
Robert Au, Harry Pavlidis and Amy Pircher, Statistics Editors

Copyright © 2020 by DIY Baseball, LLC.
All rights reserved

This book or any part thereof may not be reproduced or transmitted in any form or by any means, electronic or mechanical, including photocopying, recording, or by any information storage and retrieval system, without permission in writing from the publisher.

Limit of Liability/Disclaimer of Warranty: While the publisher and the author have used their best efforts in preparing this book, they make no representations or warranties with respect to the accuracy or completeness of the contents of this book and specifically disclaim any implied warranties of merchantability or fitness for a particular purpose. No warranty may be created or extended by sales representatives or written sales materials. The advice and strategies contained herein may not be suitable for your situation. You should consult with a professional where appropriate. Neither the publisher nor the author shall be liable for any loss of profit or any other commercial damages, including but not limited to special, incidental, consequential, or other damages.

Library of Congress Cataloging-in-Publication Data:
paperback
ISBN-13: 978-1-950716-20-3

Project Credits
Cover Design: Michael Byzewski at Aesthetic Apparatus
Interior Design and Production: Jeff Pease, Dave Pease
Layout: Jeff Pease, Dave Pease

Baseball icon courtesy of Uberux, from https://www.shareicon.net/author/uberux

Ballpark diagram courtesy of Lou Spirito/THIRTY81 Project, https://thirty81project.com/

Manufactured in the United States of America
10 9 8 7 6 5 4 3 2 1

Table of Contents

Statistical Introduction v

Part 1: Team Analysis

St. Louis Cardinals: Where Are You Going, Where Have You Been? 3
    Jeff Wiser, Jeffrey Paternostro and Matthew Trueblood

Performance Graphs 7

2019 Team Performance 8

2020 Team Projections 9

Team Personnel 10

Busch Stadium Stats 11

Cardinals Team Analysis 13

Part 2: Player Analysis

Cardinals Player Analysis 18

Cardinals Prospects 91

Part 3: Featured Articles

The Baseball Is Juiced (Again) 107
    Robert Arthur

The Moral Hazard of Playing It Safe 111
    Craig Goldstein

Index of Names 117

Statistical Introduction

Sports are, fundamentally, a blend of athletic endeavor and storytelling. Baseball, like any other sport, tells its stories in so many ways: in the arc of a game from the stands or a season from the box scores, in photos, or even in numbers. At Baseball Prospectus, we understand that statistics don't replace observation or any of baseball's stories, but complement everything else that makes the game so much fun.

What stats help us with is with patterns and precision, variance and value. This book can help you learn things you may not see from watching a game or hundred, whether it's the path of a career over time or the breadth of the entire MLB. We'd also never ask you to choose between our numbers and the experience of viewing a game from the cheap seats or the comfort of your home; our publication combines running the numbers with observations and wisdom from some of the brightest minds we can find. But if you *do* want to learn more about the numbers beyond what's on the backs of player jerseys, let us help explain.

Offense

We've revised our methodology for determining batting value. Long-time readers of the book will notice that we've retired True Average in favor of a new metric: Deserved Runs Created Plus (DRC+). Developed by Jonathan Judge and our stats team, this statistic measures everything a player does at the plate–reaching base, hitting for power, making outs, and moving runners over–and puts it on a scale where 100 equals league-average performance. A DRC+ of 150 is terrific, a DRC+ of 100 is average and a DRC+ of 75 means you better be an excellent defender.

DRC+ also does a better job than any of our previous metrics in taking contextual factors into account. The model adjusts for how the park affects performance, but also for things like the talent of the opposing pitcher, value of different types of batted-ball events, league, temperature and other factors. It's able to describe a player's expected offensive contribution than any other statistic we've found over the years, and also does a better job of predicting future performance as well.

There's a lot more to DRC+'s story, and you can read all about it in greater depth near the end of this book.

The other aspect of run-scoring is baserunning, which we quantify using Baserunning Runs. BRR not only records the value of stolen bases (or getting caught in the act), but also accounts for all the stuff that doesn't show up on the back of a baseball card: a runner's ability to go first to third on a single, or advance on a fly ball.

Defense

Where offensive value is *relatively* easy to identify and understand, defensive value is...not. Over the past dozen years, the sabermetric community has focused mostly on stats based on zone data: a real-live human person records the type of batted ball and estimated landing location, and models are created that give expected outs. From there, you can compare fielders' actual outs to those expected ones. Simple, right?

Unfortunately, zone data has two major issues. First, zone data is recorded by commercial data providers who keep the raw data private unless you pay for it. (All the statistics we build in this book and on our website use public data as inputs.) That hurts our ability to test assumptions or duplicate results. Second, over the years it has become apparent that there's quite a bit of "noise" in zone-based fielding analysis. Sometimes the conclusions drawn from zone data don't hold up to scrutiny, and sometimes the different data provided by different providers don't look anything alike, giving wildly different results. Sometimes the hard-working professional stringers or scorers might unknowingly inflict unconscious bias into the mix: for example good fielders will often be credited with more expected outs despite the data, and ballparks with high press boxes tend to score more line drives than ones with a lower press box.

Enter our Fielding Runs Above Average (FRAA). For most positions, FRAA is built from play-by-play data, which allows us to avoid the subjectivity found in many other fielding metrics. The idea is this: count how many fielding plays are made by a given player and compare that to expected plays for an average fielder at their position (based on pitcher ground ball tendencies and batter handedness). Then we adjust for park and base-out situations.

When it comes to catchers, our methodology is a little different thanks to the laundry list of responsibilities they're tasked with beyond just, well, catching and throwing the ball. By now you've probably heard about "framing" or the art of making umpires more likely to call balls outside the strike zone for strikes. To put this into one tidy number, we incorporate pitch tracking data (for the years it exists) and adjust for important factors like pitcher, umpire, batter and home-field advantage using a mixed-model approach. This grants us a number for how many strikes the catcher is personally adding to (or subtracting from) his pitchers' performance...which we then convert to runs added or lost using linear weights.

Framing is one of the biggest parts of determining catcher value, but we also take into account blocking balls from going past, whether a scorer deems it a passed ball or a wild pitch. We use a similar approach—one that really benefits from the pitch tracking data that tells us what ends up in the dirt and what doesn't. We also include a catcher's ability to prevent stolen bases and how well they field balls in play, and *finally* we come up with our FRAA for catchers.

Pitching

Both pitching and fielding make up the half of baseball that isn't run scoring: run prevention. Separating pitching from fielding is a tough task, and most recent pitching analysis has branched off from Voros McCracken's famous (and controversial) statement, "There is little if any difference among major-league pitchers in their ability to prevent hits on balls hit in the field of play." The research of the analytic community has validated this to some extent, and there are a host of "defense-independent" pitching measures that have been developed to try and extract the effect of the defense behind a hurler from the pitcher's work.

Our solution to this quandary is Deserved Run Average (DRA), our core pitching metric. DRA looks like earned run average (ERA), the tried-and-true pitching stat you've seen on every baseball broadcast or box score from the past century, but it's very different. To start, DRA takes an event-by-event look at what the pitchers does, and adjusts the value of that event based on different environmental factors like park, batter, catcher, umpire, base-out situation, run differential, inning, defense, home field advantage, pitcher role and temperature. That mixed model gives us a pitcher's expected contribution, similar to what we do for our DRC+ model for hitters and FRAA model for catchers. (Oh, and we also consider the pitcher's effect on basestealing and on balls getting past the catcher.)

It's important to note that DRA is set to the scale of runs allowed per nine innings (RA9) instead of ERA, which makes DRA's scale slightly higher than ERA's. The reason for this is because ERA tends to overrate three types of pitchers:

1. Pitchers who play in parks where scorers hand out more errors. Official scorers differ significantly in the frequency at which they assign errors to fielders.
2. Ground-ball pitchers, because a substantial proportion of errors occur on groundballs.
3. Pitchers who aren't very good. Better pitchers often allow fewer unearned runs than bad pitchers, because good pitchers tend to find ways to get out of jams.

St. Louis Cardinals 2020

Since the last time you picked up an edition of this book, we've also made a few minor changes to DRA to make it better. Recent research into "tunneling"—the act of throwing consecutive pitches that appear similar from a batter's point of view until after the swing decision point–data has given us a new contextual factor to account for in DRA: plate distance. This refers to the distance between successive pitches as they approach the plate, and while it has a smaller effect than factors like velocity or whiff rate, it still can help explain pitcher strikeout rate in our model.

New Pitching Metrics for 2020

We're including a few "new" pitching metrics in the book for the 2020 edition, though unlike last year, these numbers may be a little bit more familiar to those of you who have spent some time investigating baseball statistics.

Fastball Percentage

Our fastball percentage (FB%) statistic measures how frequently a pitcher throws a pitch classified as a "fastball," measured as a percentage of overall pitches thrown. We qualify three types of fastballs:

1. The traditional four-seam fastball;
2. The two-seam fastball or sinker;
3. "Hard cutters," which are pitches that have the movement profile of a cut fastball and are used as the pitcher's primary offering or in place of a more traditional fastball.

For example, a pitcher with a FB% of 67 throws any combination of these three pitches about two-thirds of the time.

Whiff Rate

Everybody loves a swing and a miss, and whiff rate (WHF) measures how frequently pitchers induce a swinging strike. To calculate WHF, we add up all the pitches thrown that ended with a swinging strike, then divide that number by a pitcher's total pitches thrown. Most often, high whiff rates correlate with high strikeout rates (and overall effective pitcher performance).

Called Strike Probability

Called Strike Probability (CSP) is a number that represents the likelihood that all of a pitcher's pitches will be called a strike while controlling for location, pitcher and batter handedness, umpire and count. Here's how it works: on each pitch, our model determines how many times (out of 100) that a similar pitch was called for a strike given those factors mentioned above, and when normalized for each batter's strike zone. Then we average the CSP for all pitches thrown by a pitcher in a season, and that gives us the yearly CSP percentage you see in the stats boxes.

As you might imagine, pitchers with a higher CSP are more likely to work in the zone, where pitchers with a lower CSP are likely locating their pitches outside the normal strike zone, for better or for worse.

Projections

Many of you aren't turning to this book just for a look at what a player has done, but for a look at what a player is going to do: the PECOTA projections. PECOTA, initially developed by Nate Silver (who has moved on to greater fame as a political analyst), consists of three parts:

1. Major-league equivalencies, which use minor-league statistics to project how a player will perform in the major leagues;
2. Baseline forecasts, which use weighted averages and regression to the mean to estimate a player's current true talent level; and
3. Aging curves, which uses the career paths of comparable players to estimate how a player's statistics are likely to change over time.

With all those important things covered, let's take a look at what's in the book this year.

Team Prospectus

Most of this book is composed of team chapters, with one for each of the 30 major-league franchises. On the first page of each chapter, you'll see a box that contains some of the key statistics for each team as well as a very inviting stadium diagram. (You can see an example of this for the Milwaukee Brewers on this very page!)

We start with the team name, their unadjusted 2019 win-loss record, and their divisional ranking. Beneath that are a host of other team statistics. **Pythag** presents an adjusted 2019 winning percentage, calculated by taking runs scored per game (**RS/G**) and runs allowed per game (**RA/G**) for the team, and running them through a version of Bill James' Pythagorean formula that was refined and improved by David Smyth and Brandon Heipp. (The formula is called "Pythagenpat," which is equally fun to type and to say.)

Next up is **DRC+**, described earlier, to indicate the overall hitting ability of the team either above or below league-average. Run prevention on the pitching side is covered by **DRA** (also mentioned earlier) and another metric: Fielding Independent Pitching (**FIP**), which calculates another ERA-like statistic based on strikeouts, walks, and home runs recorded. Defensive Efficiency Rating (**DER**) tells us the percentage of balls in play turned into outs for the team, and is a quick fielding shorthand that rounds out run prevention.

After that, we have several measures related to roster composition, as opposed to on-field performance. **B-Age** and **P-Age** tell us the average age of a team's batters and pitchers, respectively. **Salary** is the combined team payroll for all on-field players, and Doug Pappas' Marginal Dollars per Marginal Win (**M$/MW**) tells us how much money a team spent to earn production above replacement level.

Ending this batch of statistics is the number of disabled list days a team had over the season (**IL Days**) and the amount of salary paid to players on the disabled list (**$ on IL**); this final number is expressed as a percentage of total payroll.

Next to each of these stats, we've listed each team's MLB rank in that category from first to 30th. In this, first always indicates a positive outcome and 30th a negative outcome, except in the case of salary—first is highest.

After the franchise statistics, we share a few items about the team's home ballpark. There's the aforementioned diagram of the park's dimensions (including distances to the outfield wall), a graphic showing the height of the wall from the left-field pole to the right-field pole, and a table showing three-year park factors for the stadium. The park factors are displayed as indexes where 100 is average, 110 means that the park inflates the statistic in question by 10 percent, and 90 means that the park deflates the statistic in question by 10 percent.

On the second page of each team chapter, you'll find three graphs. The first is the **2019 Hit List Ranking**. This shows our Hit List Rank for the team on each day of the 2019 season and is intended to give you a picture of the ups and downs of the team's season. Hit List Rank measures overall team performance and drives the Hit List Power Rankings at the baseballprospectus.com website.

The second graph is **Committed Payroll** and helps you see how the team's payroll has compared to the MLB and divisional average payrolls over time. Payroll figures are current as of January 1, 2020; with so many free agents still unsigned as of this writing, the final 2020 figure will likely be significantly different for many teams. (In the meantime, you can always find the most current data at Baseball Prospectus' Cot's Baseball Contracts page.)

The third graph is **Farm System Ranking** and displays how the Baseball Prospectus prospect team has ranked the organization's farm system since 2007.

After the graphs, we have a **Personnel** section that lists many of the important decision-makers and upper-level field and operations staff members for the franchise, as well as any former Baseball Prospectus staff members who are currently part of the organization. (In very rare circumstances, someone might be on both lists!)

www.baseballprospectus.com

Juan Soto LF
Born: 10/25/98 Age: 21 Bats: L Throws: L
Height: 6'1" Weight: 185 Origin: International Free Agent, 2015

YEAR	TEAM	LVL	AGE	PA	R	2B	3B	HR	RBI	BB	K	SB	CS	AVG/OBP/SLG
2017	NAT	RK	18	27	3	1	1	0	4	2	1	0	0	.320/.370/.440
2017	HAG	A	18	96	15	5	0	3	14	10	8	1	2	.360/.427/.523
2018	HAG	A	19	74	12	5	3	5	24	14	13	2	0	.373/.486/.814
2018	POT	A+	19	73	17	3	1	7	18	11	8	0	1	.371/.466/.790
2018	HAR	AA	19	35	4	2	0	2	10	4	7	1	0	.323/.400/.581
2018	WAS	MLB	19	494	77	25	1	22	70	79	99	5	2	.292/.406/.517
2019	WAS	MLB	20	659	110	32	5	34	110	108	132	12	1	.282/.401/.548
2020	WAS	MLB	21	630	92	30	3	35	102	85	123	5	2	.284/.382/.543

Comparables: Ronald Acuña Jr., Mike Trout, Tony Conigliaro

YEAR	TEAM	LVL	AGE	PA	DRC+	VORP	BABIP	BRR	FRAA	WARP
2017	NAT	RK	18	27	135	1.5	.333	0.0	RF(9): -1.1	0.0
2017	HAG	A	18	96	181	8.0	.373	1.0	RF(19): -1.9, LF(2): -0.3	0.9
2018	HAG	A	19	74	222	14.5	.405	0.3	RF(14): 1.1, CF(2): 0.2	1.2
2018	POT	A+	19	73	260	15.4	.340	1.4	RF(14): 1.0, LF(1): 0.0	1.6
2018	HAR	AA	19	35	113	3.6	.364	0.0	LF(4): 0.6, RF(4): -0.5	0.1
2018	WAS	MLB	19	494	125	40.5	.338	-0.5	LF(114): 2.7	3.0
2019	WAS	MLB	20	659	136	49.0	.312	1.4	LF(150): -0.8	4.9
2020	WAS	MLB	21	630	133	43.6	.310	-0.1	LF 3	4.8

Position Players

After all that information and a thoughtful bylined essay covering each team, we present our player comments. These are also bylined, but due to frequent franchise shifts during the offseason, our bylines are more a rough guide than a perfect accounting of who wrote what.

Each player is listed with the major-league team that employed him as of early January 2020. If a player changed teams after that point via free agency, trade, or any other method, you'll be able to find them in the chapter for their previous squad.

As an example, take a look at the player comment for Nationals outfielder Juan Soto: the stat block that accompanies his written comment is at the top of this page. First we cover biographical information (age is as of June 30, 2020) before moving onto the stats themselves. Our statistic columns include standard identifying information like **YEAR**, **TEAM**, **LVL** (level of affiliated play) and **AGE** before getting into the numbers. Next, we provide raw, untranslated numbers like you might find on the back of your dad's baseball cards: **PA** (plate appearances), **R** (runs), **2B** (doubles), **3B** (triples), **HR** (home runs), **RBI** (runs batted in), **BB** (walks), **K** (strikeouts), **SB** (stolen bases) and **CS** (caught stealing).

Statistical Introduction - xi

Next, we have unadjusted "slash" statistics: **AVG** (batting average), **OBP** (on-base percentage) and **SLG** (slugging percentage). Following the slash line is **DRC+** (Deserved Runs Created Plus), which we described earlier as total offensive expected contribution compared to the league average.

One of our oldest active metrics, **VORP** (Value Over Replacement Player), considers offensive production, position and plate appearances. In essence, it is the number of runs contributed beyond what a replacement-level player at the same position would contribute if given the same percentage of team plate appearances. VORP does not consider the quality of a player's defense.

BABIP (batting average on balls in play) tells us how often a ball in play fell for a hit, and can help us identify whether a batter may have been lucky or not...but note that high BABIPs also tend to follow the great hitters of our time, as well as speedy singles hitters who put the ball on the ground.

The next item is **BRR** (Baserunning Runs), which covers all of a player's baserunning accomplishments including (but not limited to) swiped bags and failed attempts. Next is **FRAA** (Fielding Runs Above Average), which also includes the number of games previously played at each position noted in parentheses. Multi-position players have only their two most frequent positions listed here, but their total FRAA number reflects all positions played.

Our last column here is **WARP** (Wins Above Replacement Player). WARP estimates the total value of a player, which means for hitters it takes into account hitting runs above average (calculated using the DRC+ model), BRR and FRAA. Then, it makes an adjustment for positions played and gives the player a credit for plate appearances based upon the difference between "replacement level"—which is derived from the quality of players added to a team's roster after the start of the season–and the league average.

The final line just below the stats box is **PECOTA** data, which is discussed further in a following section.

Catchers

Catchers are a special breed, and thus they have earned their own separate box which displays some of the defensive metrics that we've built just for them. As an example, let's check out J.T. Realmuto.

The **YEAR** and **TEAM** columns match what you'd find in the other stat box. **P. COUNT** indicates the number of pitches thrown while the catcher was behind the plate, including swinging strikes, fouls and balls in play. **FRM RUNS** is the total run value the catcher provided (or cost) his team by influencing the umpire to call strikes where other catchers did not. **BLK RUNS** expresses the total run value above or below average for the catcher's ability to prevent wild pitches and passed balls. **THRW RUNS** is calculated using a similar model as the previous two statistics, and it measures a catcher's ability to throw out basestealers but also to dissuade them from testing his arm in the first place. It takes into account factors like the pitcher (including his delivery and pickoff move) and baserunner (who could be as fast as Billy Hamilton or as slow as Yonder Alonso). **TOT RUNS** is the sum of all of the previous three statistics.

Justin Verlander   RHP

Born: 02/20/83   Age: 37   Bats: R   Throws: R
Height: 6'5"   Weight: 225   Origin: Round 1, 2004 Draft (#2 overall)

YEAR	TEAM	LVL	AGE	W	L	SV	G	GS	IP	H	HR	BB/9	K/9	K	GB%	BABIP
2017	DET	MLB	34	10	8	0	28	28	172	153	23	3.5	9.2	176	34%	.283
2017	HOU	MLB	34	5	0	0	5	5	34	17	4	1.3	11.4	43	32%	.194
2018	HOU	MLB	35	16	9	0	34	34	214	156	28	1.6	12.2	290	31%	.272
2019	HOU	MLB	36	21	6	0	34	34	223	137	36	1.7	12.1	300	36%	.219
2020	HOU	MLB	37	15	6	0	29	29	184	138	28	2.3	12.1	248	35%	.274

Comparables: Zack Greinke, A.J. Burnett, Aníbal Sánchez

YEAR	TEAM	LVL	AGE	WHIP	ERA	DRA	WARP	MPH	FB%	WHF	CSP
2017	DET	MLB	34	1.28	3.82	4.03	3.0	97.7	58	11	47.8
2017	HOU	MLB	34	0.65	1.06	3.08	0.9	97.5	59.6	15.1	49.9
2018	HOU	MLB	35	0.90	2.52	2.33	7.3	97.5	61.2	16.2	51.6
2019	HOU	MLB	36	0.80	2.58	2.51	7.9	96.8	49.9	17.5	48.3
2020	HOU	MLB	37	1.01	2.75	2.95	5.3	95.8	54.6	15.1	48.2

Pitchers

Let's give our pitchers a turn, using 2019 AL Cy Young winner Justin Verlander as our example. Take a look at his stat block: the first line and the **YEAR**, **TEAM**, **LVL** and **AGE** columns are the same as in the position player example earlier.

Here too, we have a series of columns that display raw, unadjusted statistics compiled by the pitcher over the course of a season: **W** (wins), **L** (losses), **SV** (saves), **G** (games pitched), **GS** (games started), **IP** (innings pitched), **H** (hits allowed) and **HR** (home runs allowed). Next we have two statistics that are rates: **BB/9** (walks per nine innings) and **K/9** (strikeouts per nine innings), before returning to the unadjusted K (strikeouts).

Next up is **GB%** (ground ball percentage), which is the percentage of all batted balls that were hit on the ground, including both outs and hits. Remember, this is based on observational data and subject to human error, so please approach this with a healthy dose of skepticism.

BABIP (batting average on balls in play) is calculated using the same methodology as it is for position players, but it often tells us more about a pitcher than it does a hitter. With pitchers, a high BABIP is often due to poor defense or bad luck, and can often be an indicator of potential rebound, and a low BABIP may be cause to expect performance regression. (A typical league-average BABIP is close to .290-.300.)

The metrics **WHIP** (walks plus hits per inning pitched) and **ERA** (earned run average) are old standbys: WHIP measures walks and hits allowed on a per-inning basis, while ERA measures earned runs on a nine-inning basis. Neither of these stats are translated or adjusted.

DRA (Deserved Run Average) was described at length earlier, and measures how many runs the pitcher "deserved" to allow per nine innings. Please note that since we lack all the data points that would make for a "real" DRA for minor-league events, the DRA displayed for minor league partial-seasons is based off of different data. (That data is a modified version of our cFIP metric, which you can find more information about on our website.)

Just like with hitters, **WARP** (Wins Above Replacement Player) is a total value metric that puts pitchers of all stripes on the same scale as position players. We use DRA as the primary input for our calculation of WARP. You might notice that relief pitchers (due to their limited innings) may have a lower WARP than you were expecting or than you might see in other WARP-like metrics. WARP does not take leverage into account, just the actions a pitcher performs and the expected value of those actions...which ends up judging high-leverage relief pitchers differently than you might imagine given their prestige and market value.

MPH gives you the pitcher's 95th percentile velocity for the noted season, in order to give you an idea of what the *peak* fastball velocity a pitcher possesses. Since this comes from our pitch-tracking data, it is not publicly available for minor-league pitchers.

Finally, we display the three new pitching metrics we described earlier. **FB%** (fastball percentage) gives you the percentage of fastballs thrown out of all pitches. **WHF** (whiff rate) tells you the percentage of swinging strikes induced out of all pitches. **CSP** (called strike probability) expresses the likelihood of all pitches thrown to result in a called strike, after controlling for factors like handedness, umpire, pitch type, count and location.

PECOTA

All players have PECOTA projections for 2020, as well as a set of other numbers that describe the performance of comparable players according to PECOTA. All projections for 2020 are for the player at the date we went to press in early January and are projected into the league and park context as indicated by the team abbreviation. (Note that players at very low levels of the minors are too unpredictable to assess using these numbers.) All PECOTA projected statistics represent a player's projected major-league performance.

Below the projections are the player's three highest-scoring comparable players as determined by PECOTA. All comparables represent a snapshot of how the listed player was performing at the same age as the current player, so if a

23-year-old pitcher is compared to Bartolo Colón, he's actually being compared to a 23-year-old Colón, not the version that pitched for the Rangers in 2018, nor to Colón's career as a whole.

A few points about pitcher projections. First, we aren't yet projecting peak velocity, so that column will be blank in the PECOTA lines. Second, projecting DRA is trickier than evaluating past performance, because it is unclear how deserving each pitcher will be of his anticipated outcomes. However, we know that another DRA-related statistic–contextual FIP or cFIP-estimates future run scoring very well. So for PECOTA, the projected DRA figures you see are based on the past cFIPs generated by the pitcher and comparable players over time, along with the other factors described above.

Lineouts

In each chapter's Lineouts section, you'll find abbreviated text comments, as well as all the same information you'd find in our full player comments. The only difference is that we limit the stats boxes in this section to only including the 2019 information for each player.

Managers

After all those wonderful team chapters, we've got statistics for each big-league manager, all of whom are organized by alphabetical order. Here you'll find a block including an extraordinary amount of information collected from each manager's entire career. For more information on the acronyms and what they mean, please visit the Glossary at www.baseballprospectus.com.

There is one important metric that we'd like to call attention to, and you'll find it next to each manager's name: **wRM+** (weighted reliever management plus). Developed by Rob Arthur and Rian Watt, wRM+ investigates how good a manager is at using their best relievers during the moments of highest leverage, using both our proprietary DRA metric as well as Leverage Index. wRM+ is scaled to a league average of 100, and a wRM+ of 105 indicates that relievers were used approximately five percent "better" than average. On the other hand, a wRM+ of 95 would tell us the team used its relievers five percent "worse" than the average team.

While wRM+ does not have an extremely strong correlation with a manager, it is statistically significant; this means that a manager is not *entirely* responsible for a team's wRM+, but does have some effect on that number.

PECOTA Leaderboards

If you're familiar with PECOTA, then you'll have noticed that the projection system often appears bullish on players coming off a bad year and bearish on players coming off a good year. (This is because the system weights several previous seasons, not just the most recent one.) In addition, we publish the 50th percentile projections for each player–which is smack in the middle of the range of projected production—which tends to mean PECOTA stat lines don't often have extreme results like 40 home runs or 250 strikeouts in a given season. In essence, PECOTA doesn't project very many extreme seasons.

At the end of the book, we've ranked the top players at each position based on their PECOTA projections. This might help you visualize just how a given player's projection compares to that of their peers, so that even if a dramatic stat line isn't projected, you can still imagine how they stack up against the rest of the league.

Part 1: Team Analysis

St. Louis Cardinals: Where Are You Going, Where Have You Been?

Jeff Wiser, Jeffrey Paternostro and Matthew Trueblood

2019: What Went Right

What a year to be a Cardinals fan. The team defied the odds and expectations to take control of a murky National League Central—a precarious division without a clear-cut leader. In mid-July, with their record at .500 and the Cubs and Brewers hovering above them, their playoff odds fell below 20 percent. By mid-August, those odds rose above 50 percent. While the Cubs posed a threat until late in the season and the Brewers put on a late push, the Cardinals refused to cede the momentum they gained over the summer en route to taking the division crown and reaching the NLCS. Following that 45-45 start, the Cardinals went 46-26 (.639). It was the third-best record in the league after those of the Dodgers and Mets.

How they did it was surprising. St. Louis didn't slug their way to the top, but their position-player crop did the little things to push the team forward. Their biggest calling card might have been infield defense. The Cards led baseball in converting double play opportunities into twin-killings thanks to an up-the-middle combination of Kolten Wong and Paul DeJong. The addition of Paul Goldschmidt, a long-time leader in first-base defense thanks to his ability to start double plays, added fuel to the infield fire. The team's entire defense was fourth in baseball in defensive efficiency.

On the flip side, they were a top-ten team in avoiding hitting into double plays and were very effective on the bases overall. They were near the top of the league in advancing on fly balls that were caught for outs and tied for third in the majors in stolen bases. Add it all up and the team entered October as the best baserunning team in the playoffs.

The rotation was good, if not truly outstanding. Jack Flaherty cemented himself as one of the premier young arms in the game by posting a 2.75 ERA and 231 strikeouts over 33 starts and 196 1/3 innings of work. Miles Mikolas backed

Flaherty up nicely, as did Dakota Hudson, while veteran Adam Wainwright took his turn every fifth day and provided quality starting depth. The rotation accounted for the highest ground ball rate among all starting groups, helping to avoid some of the zoom ball's nasty side effects while playing right into the hands of their excellent infield defense.

The bullpen, as a unit, was spectacular. Cards relievers ended the regular season with the sixth-best ERA in the game and the second-best DRA. After flame-throwing Jordan Hicks shredded his elbow ligament, erstwhile starter Carlos Martínez took over the closer role and acquitted himself well. Giovanny Gallegos was a revelation in his first full big-league season, striking out 93 batters and walking just 16 over 74 innings. John Brebbia, Tyler Webb, and John Gant were solid middle relief options for Mike Shildt, forming a reliable bridge from the starters to Gallegos and Martínez down the stretch.. The entire pitching staff—starters and relievers combined—allowed the third-fewest home runs on the year.

2019: What Went Wrong

As good as the collective pitching staff was, the offense never really caught fire. The team's hitters had a collective DRC+ of just 93 on the year, tied with the Blue Jays, Reds, and Rockies for 18th-best in baseball. The team's best hitter was Goldschmidt, but he had the worst offensive season of his career. Marcell Ozuna, Dexter Fowler and Matt Carpenter also disappointed. Tommy Edman filled Carpenter's shoes surprisingly well, but one breakout couldn't erase a quartet of flops. Only three NL teams hit fewer home runs and the Cardinals hit the seventh-fewest in the majors overall.

The Cardinals' starters were below-average in strikeout rate and had the eighth-highest walk rate in baseball. They got away with all of the batted balls thanks to their stellar defense, but that defensive dependence paints a picture of a precarious future—balls in play don't always find their way into even the best of gloves. The bullpen lost Hicks to a torn UCL and Alex Reyes saw limited action before his season was ended (again) by injury. What the Cardinals can get from that talented pair in 2020 seems up in the air at best. *—Jeff Wiser*

Prospect Outlook

Any analysis of what Cardinals prospects might help the 2020 version of the team is going to end up mostly useless, or at least quickly dated. Witness Edman, who began the year as a useful, if overage, super-utility prospect, the kind most systems—including the Cardinals—have lurking in the fourth or fifth tier of their farm. He swatted 18 bombs in a shade under 600 PA, most of which were in the majors. Edman—a sixth-round college bat less than four years ago—handled five different positions and hit .300 with power in the majors.

Dylan Carlson's breakout was easier to foresee, given his amateur pedigree. He struggled in his first full pro season in 2018, admittedly in tough hitting environments, but the athleticism jumped, the swing got tweaked, and he destroyed the upper minors while playing a competent center field. He'll have a case as the best prospect in the system over third baseman **Nolan Gorman**, who was no slouch with the bat himself as a 19-year old across two A-ball levels. That's top-tier talent at the top of the system, and they are joined by polished college lefty **Zack Thompson**, the 19th-overall pick in this past summer's draft, but beyond that, it's a lot of third base profiles and the next recipients of the Cardinals' brand of player development devil-magic—let's say **Conner Capel** and **Seth Elledge** (for entertainment purposes only). —*Jeffrey Paternostro*

2020 Outlook

For a team with a clear path to a second-straight division title, but also one with clear flaws and an eyebrow-raising aging profile, the Cardinals were shockingly inactive over the winter. Ownership left little in the way of financial flexibility, but rather than try to create something and fish seriously in the deep free-agent waters, President of Baseball Ops John Mozeliak and GM Mike Girsch emphasized quiet dependability. They re-signed Wainwright to another incentive-heavy deal and plan to have him slot into their rotation again. He'll be joined there by Kwang-hyun Kim, a Korean southpaw with the deep arsenal and the command-first profile the team still prizes. They also retained Matt Wieters, fortifying (rather than clearing) the logjam keeping Andrew Knizner from seeing consistent time in the majors.

In the outfield, however, they were markedly youth-friendly. José Martínez and Randy Arozarena went to Tampa Bay in a trade for top-echelon pitching prospect Matthew Liberatore, but rather than re-sign Ozuna or pursue Nick Castellanos, Mozeliak announced that the deal paved the way to more playing time for Edman, Bader, Thomas, Tyler O'Neill, and (eventually, implicitly) Carlson. Unless and until a couple of those players prove they can be consistent and above-average regulars, however, there remain some obvious holes in the lineup. The Cardinals could easily repeat as division champions, but it feels like they missed a clear opportunity to do more. —*Matthew Trueblood*

Performance Graphs

2019 Hit List Ranking

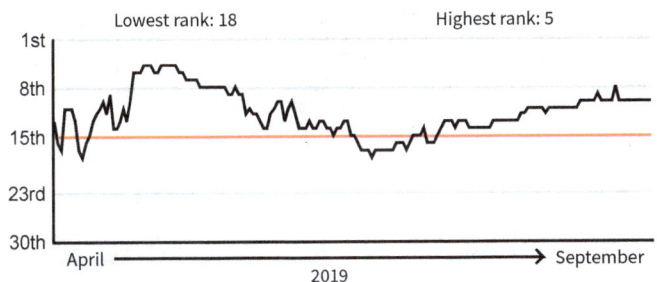

Committed Payroll (in millions)

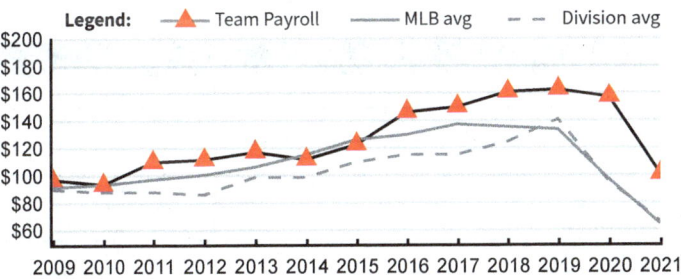

Farm System Ranking

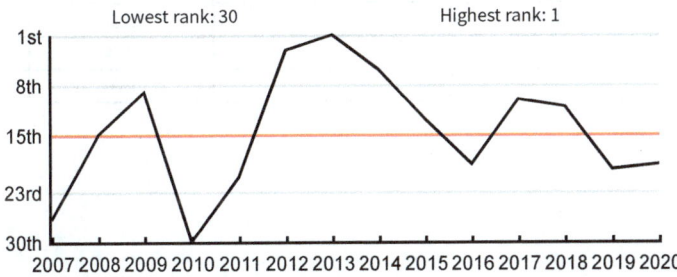

2019 Team Performance

ACTUAL STANDINGS

Team	W	L	Pct
SLN	91	71	0.562
MIL	89	73	0.549
CHN	84	78	0.519
CIN	75	87	0.463
PIT	69	93	0.426

THIRD-ORDER STANDINGS

Team	W	L	Pct
SLN	91	71	0.564
CHN	88	74	0.543
MIL	87	75	0.535
CIN	86	76	0.534
PIT	66	96	0.407

TOP HITTERS

Player	WARP
Paul DeJong	4.2
Kolten Wong	4.1
Harrison Bader	2.5

TOP PITCHERS

Player	WARP
Jack Flaherty	7.1
Miles Mikolas	3.3
Dakota Hudson	2.4

VITAL STATISTICS

Statistic Name	Value	Rank
Pythagenpat	.566	10th
Runs Scored per Game	4.72	19th
Runs Allowed per Game	4.09	5th
Deserved Runs Created Plus	93	18th
Deserved Run Average	4.19	6th
Fielding Independent Pitching	4.22	11th
Defensive Efficiency Rating	.717	5th
Batter Age	29.0	28th
Pitcher Age	27.8	11th
Salary	$162.6M	7th
Marginal $ per Marginal Win	$3.5M	18th
Injured List Days	924	7th
$ on IL	15%	16th

2020 Team Projections

PROJECTED STANDINGS

Team	W	L	Pct	+/-
CIN	86.1	75.9	0.531	11
CHN	84.5	77.5	0.522	0
SLN	**80.3**	**81.7**	**0.496**	**-11**
MIL	79.4	82.6	0.490	-10
PIT	70.3	91.7	0.434	1

TOP PROJECTED HITTERS

Player	WARP
Paul Goldschmidt	3.5
Kolten Wong	3.0
Harrison Bader	2.9

TOP PROJECTED PITCHERS

Player	WARP
Jack Flaherty	4.8
Carlos Martínez	1.5
Giovanny Gallegos	1.4

FARM SYSTEM REPORT

Top Prospect	Number of Top 101 Prospects
Dylan Carlson, #18	2

KEY DEDUCTIONS

Player	WARP
Marcell Ozuna	1.9
José Martínez	0.9
Michael Wacha	0.9
Randy Arozarena	0.3
Ramón Urías	0.0
Adolis García	0.0
Mike Mayers	-0.2

KEY ADDITIONS

Player	WARP
Brad Miller	0.9
Dylan Carlson	0.5
Austin Dean	0.3
Kodi Whitley	0.1
Jake Woodford	0.0
Alvaro Seijas	-0.2
Elehuris Montero	-0.4
Kwang-Hyun Kim	-0.7

Team Personnel

President of Baseball Operations
John Mozeliak

Vice President & General Manager
Mike Girsch

Assistant General Manager
Moises Rodriguez

Assistant General Manager & Director of Scouting
Randy Flores

Manager
Mike Shildt

BP Alumni
Zach Mortimer
Christopher Rodriguez
Mauricio Rubio

Busch Stadium Stats

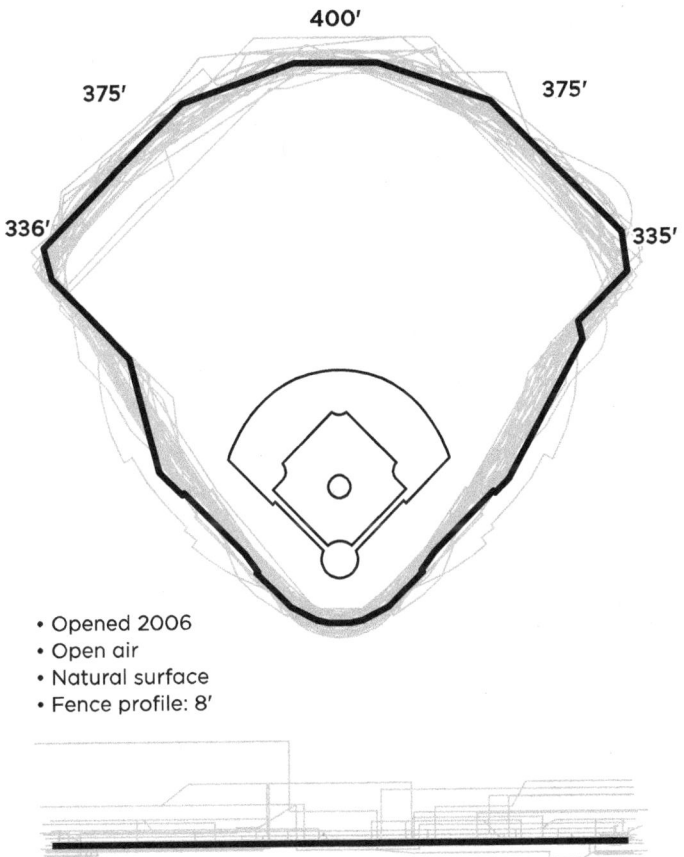

- Opened 2006
- Open air
- Natural surface
- Fence profile: 8'

Three-Year Park Factors

Runs	Runs/RH	Runs/LH	HR/RH	HR/LH
96	96	96	91	98

Cardinals Team Analysis

We know better than to ever count out the Cardinals. But still, St. Louis' rise back to the top of the National League Central in 2019 over the Brewers and Cubs was mildly surprising given Chicago or Milwaukee had won the division in each of the previous three years. It was even more surprising considering that first baseman Paul Goldschmidt and third baseman Matt Carpenter—two of the Cardinals' best and most important hitters—had down seasons.

In his first season with the Cards, Goldschmidt got off to a very slow start. He eventually rebounded, but ended up posting the lowest full-season OPS of his career (.821). Carpenter, on the other hand, experienced an abrupt decline; just a year after setting career-highs in homers (36) and OPS (.897), he hit .226/.334/.392 and spent most of October on the bench.

Goldschmidt is about to enter his age-32 season, while Carpenter is going on his age-34 campaign. Given they didn't perform up to their normal standards in 2019 and St. Louis ended up in the National League Championship Series, it's fair to ask—are these two still instrumental in the Cardinals' success, or can the team win without significant contributions from them? And, on top of that: is there any reason to believe that rebound seasons could be in order?

⚾ ⚾ ⚾

The answer to the first pay may lie in how the Cardinals captured the division crown last year and how different things were from '18. That's because the two key areas in which the Cardinals significantly improved, somewhat mitigating the lineup's mediocre offensive performance, were the defense and the bullpen.

Let's start with the defensive improvement, because it actually has something to do with Goldschmidt. Adding the three-time Gold Glove first baseman in place of José Martínez, who made 84 starts at first in '18, drastically improved St. Louis' glovework at the cold corner. Consider that on a team level, the Cardinals converted 76.8 percent of grounders into outs in 2018—good for 11th in the majors. Last season, that percentage improved to 78.8 percent—or the second-highest mark in the majors.

Goldschmidt undoubtedly played a role in that improvement, though he wasn't alone in that regard. Staying on the right side of the infield, better health and stronger production at the plate kept Kolten Wong at second base for 147 games, and it resulted in his first career Gold Glove Award. Meanwhile, the

Cardinals received a boost from rookie Tommy Edman, who proved to be a defensive upgrade over Carpenter at the hot corner in his 55 appearances there. The difference between the two, per FRAA, was worth nearly 10 runs.

The Cardinals were better at turning balls hit in the air into outs, too, with the fleet-of-foot Harrison Bader playing in 48 more games in center field than he did in '18. Bader finished 10th in baseball (minimum 300 plate appearances) in FRAA, joining Wong (sixth) as the only pair of teammates to rank so high.

Defense certainly helps pitching, but so does...well, better pitching. The Cardinals' bullpen ranked second in the majors in DRA last season, a wide improvement over 2018, when they ranked 26th. That leap would have been impressive regardless, but it came during a season in which St. Louis received just 28 innings from closer Jordan Hicks before he was lost to injury.

The Cardinals received a huge lift foremost from Giovanny Gallegos, who was acquired from the Yankees in summer 2018 as part of the Luke Voit trade. He appeared more frequently in 2019, and for good reason: he posted a 2.31 ERA and struck out 33 percent of the batters he faced in 74 innings. Gallegos' unique mix of a slightly-above-average four-seam fastball with rise and a pitch he calls a slider but doesn't really act like one—it actually moves horizontally—can be tough for a hitter to distinguish. Hence the high K rate and excellent results when the ball was put in play against him—opposing batters hit .170.

The Cards made Carlos Martinez their closer after Hicks got hurt, and it worked—he finished with a 3.17 ERA over 48 relief appearances overall. Martinez will likely get a shot to return to the rotation in 2020, but between Gallegos and right-hander Ryan Helsley, who posted a 2.95 ERA over 24 appearances last season, and even Andrew Miller and John Brebbia, St. Louis has some late-inning options in throw out there ahead of Hicks' eventual return.

It would seem to bode well for the Cardinals that all the important actors in their run-prevention improvement—including the major one in the rotation we didn't address, in Jack Flaherty—will be in place for the 2020 season as well.

⚾ ⚾ ⚾

And then there are the two veteran sluggers we opened with, Goldschmidt and Carpenter. We've seen why the Cardinals were able to win despite subpar years from these two, but is there hope for a bounceback for either and/or both going into the 2020 season?

Let's start with a look at Goldschmidt. On July 1st of last season, he was hitting .246/.336/.405. He got red-hot in July, slugging 11 homers while slashing .308/.360/.725. He tapered off the rest of the way, posting a .259/.354/.472 line with nine homers over the final two months. But if you look at his quality of contact year-over-year from 2018-19, you'll find that while his surface-level stats were down significantly, his batted-ball profile wasn't far off from where it was when he turned in a more Goldy-like .922 OPS.

Goldschmidt's hard-hit rate, according to Statcast (percentage of batted balls with an exit velocity 95 mph or greater), was nearly identical to what it was in 2018—it was 43.8 percent then, and 42.4 percent last year. Likewise, while he barreled-up the baseball at a lower rate in '19, the discrepancy isn't super large—13.6 percent of batted balls to 11.3 percent.

Goldschmidt's DRC+ declined from 136 to 119, but while that gap certainly looks concerning, the differential in his Statcast expected weighted on-base average (based on launch angle and exit velocity of batted balls) wasn't as wretched (.384 to .361). And, while his .476 slugging percentage last year was the lowest for any full season of his career, his expected slugging percentage was 37 points higher.

Goldschmidt's average exit velocity was 90.1 mph in 2019, down 0.7 mph from '18. His average launch angle was nearly identical, at 15.3 degrees following a season in which it was 15.7. Now, that's all well and good when Goldschmidt makes contact—perhaps there is reason for optimism that 2019 was an aberration and not the start of a broader decline. But what about when he doesn't? His K rate was actually a smidge lower than in '18, down from 25.1 percent to 24.3 percent. He did walk a bit less, however, with his walk rate declining from 13.8 percent to 11.4 percent.

The quality of contact and plate-discipline figures indicate Goldschmidt lost his way early in his first season with a new club, but remains the hitter he had been in prior years—one who is regularly in the NL Most Valuable Player conversation (though he has yet to win). The Cardinals sure hope those indicators prove correct—after all, they inked Goldschmidt to a long-term extension that will run through the 2024 season before he'd even played a game with them.

⚾ ⚾ ⚾

So what about Carpenter, who had a career year at the plate in '18?

While Goldschmidt's quality of contact and strikeout rate suggest he did not fall off in his performance as much as his 101-point loss in OPS would indicate, the opposite appears to be true for Carpenter.

Carpenter's hard-hit rate was down drastically, from 44.7 percent to 31.1 percent, ranking 185th out of the 223 hitters who had put at least 250 balls in play last season. (He ranked 32nd out of 228 hitters in that category in 2018.) His barrel rate was sliced nearly in half, down from 13.7 percent to 7.8 percent. His groundball rate went from 28.3 percent to 34.5 percent. The strikeout rate went up from 23.3 percent to 26.1 percent, and the walk rate was down for the usually patient and discerning Carpenter, from 15.1 percent to 12.8 percent.

This is all bad. But wait, there's more.

As strong of a season as Carpenter had in 2018, there are some trends that suggest it was more likely an outlier than an indication of an output level he'll return to and sustain. Take, for example, his hard-hit rate in '17, before the big season at the plate—it was 37 percent, much more in line with what it was in '19 than the 44.7 percent from '18. And the barrel rate illustrates this point more vividly—it was 8.2 percent in '17, nearly the same as the 7.8 percent barrel rate in '19, with his big season sandwiched in the middle.

Furthermore, Carpenter's strikeout rate has been increasing progressively over the last three seasons, even including his career year in '18. It's climbed six percentage points. Predictably, his chase rate has also been rising, going from 14.3 percent in '17, to 18.4 percent in '18, to 20.7 percent last year. And before it jumped to 135 in '18, Carpenter's DRC+ was progressively declining, from 133 in 2015, to 126 in '16, to 119 in '17. It was 96 last year. That dropped Carpenter from 14th in baseball among qualifiers in '18 to out of the top 100.

So, is this it for Carpenter? Have we seen his best baseball? At minimum, those trends aren't encouraging.

⚾ ⚾ ⚾

Even if things don't change with Carpenter and Goldschmidt, what the Cardinals have going for them is history; they've shown they can weather a subpar season from both and still win the division—that their balanced roster can overcome an absent or underperforming star.

In that sense, last season was the ultimate throwback season for the Cardinals, who we should once again be careful about counting out.

—Manny Randhawa is a writer and Statcast researcher for MLB.com.

Part 2: Player Analysis

PLAYER COMMENTS WITH GRAPHS

Harrison Bader CF
Born: 06/03/94 Age: 26 Bats: R Throws: R
Height: 6'0" Weight: 195 Origin: Round 3, 2015 Draft (#100 overall)

YEAR	TEAM	LVL	AGE	PA	R	2B	3B	HR	RBI	BB	K	SB	CS	AVG/OBP/SLG
2017	MEM	AAA	23	479	74	18	1	20	55	34	118	15	9	.283/.347/.469
2017	SLN	MLB	23	92	10	3	0	3	10	5	24	2	1	.235/.283/.376
2018	SLN	MLB	24	427	61	20	2	12	37	31	125	15	3	.264/.334/.422
2019	MEM	AAA	25	75	23	3	0	7	15	8	16	3	0	.317/.427/.698
2019	SLN	MLB	25	406	54	14	3	12	39	46	117	11	3	.205/.314/.366
2020	SLN	MLB	26	427	51	17	2	17	55	36	125	11	5	.234/.317/.423

Comparables: Kirk Nieuwenhuis, Derek Fisher, Jackie Bradley Jr.

Outfield defense is hard to judge. Watching on TV, you never see the positioning or the jump, only the end of the play. Was that dive necessary, or did it make up for a bad jump? Was that ball uncatchable, or did the fielder take a bad route? That's all unknowable. And yet, watch Bader play outfield, and it's clear that he's superb. He takes protractor-straight routes, gets up to full speed quickly, and finishes plays with aplomb. He has a cannon arm, too, in case you judge outfielders by their assists. And yet, despite being maybe the best defensive outfielder in baseball, Bader's bat required a minor-league stint in 2019. He doesn't need to hit to be a valuable contributor, but the Cardinals are right to spend time working on his offense. If he can just flirt with a league-average line, he'd be one of the most valuable outfielders in the game.

YEAR	TEAM	LVL	AGE	PA	DRC+	VORP	BABIP	BRR	FRAA	WARP
2017	MEM	AAA	23	479	117	41.2	.345	5.3	CF(111): 13.7, RF(3): 0.3	4.5
2017	SLN	MLB	23	92	82	1.2	.288	0.3	CF(20): 2.0, LF(7): -0.1	0.3
2018	SLN	MLB	24	427	90	25.1	.358	2.8	CF(74): 9.1, RF(38): 1.6	2.2
2019	MEM	AAA	25	75	158	14.8	.325	1.4	CF(15): 1.7	1.0
2019	SLN	MLB	25	406	84	6.6	.268	4.5	CF(122): 14.4	2.5
2020	SLN	MLB	26	427	99	17.2	.301	1.7	CF 12	3.0

Harrison Bader, continued

Batted Ball Distribution

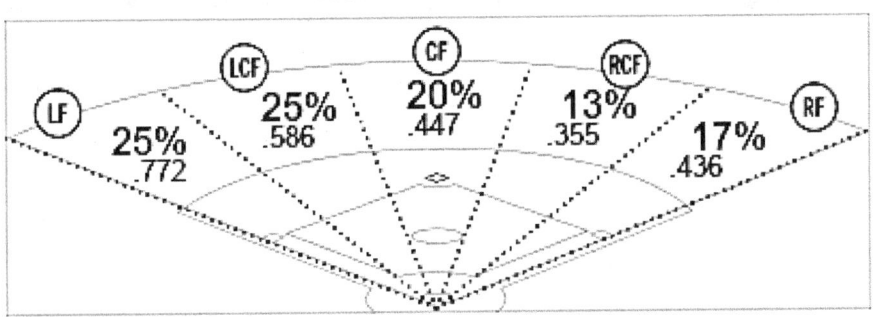

| Strike Zone vs LHP | Strike Zone vs RHP |

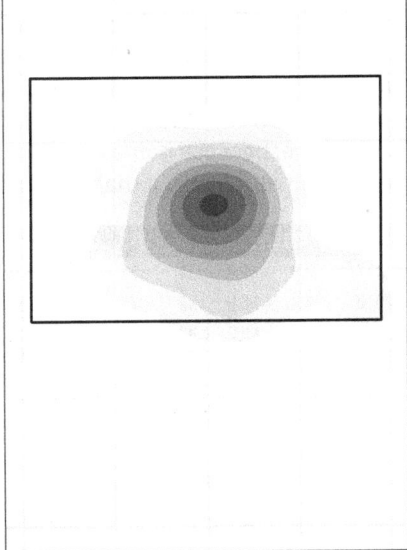

Matt Carpenter 3B

Born: 11/26/85 Age: 34 Bats: L Throws: R
Height: 6'3" Weight: 205 Origin: Round 13, 2009 Draft (#399 overall)

YEAR	TEAM	LVL	AGE	PA	R	2B	3B	HR	RBI	BB	K	SB	CS	AVG/OBP/SLG
2017	SLN	MLB	31	622	91	31	2	23	69	109	125	2	1	.241/.384/.451
2018	SLN	MLB	32	677	111	42	0	36	81	102	158	4	1	.257/.374/.523
2019	SLN	MLB	33	492	59	20	2	15	46	63	129	6	1	.226/.334/.392
2020	SLN	MLB	34	469	56	21	2	17	58	65	122	3	1	.227/.342/.417

Comparables: Brian Dozier, Dan Uggla, Kelly Johnson

Carpenter has continually reinvented himself; he came up as a high-contact, slap-hitting utility infielder and turned himself into an ultra-patient slugging first baseman. Last year's transformation (if you can call it that) was something new—he became a below-average hitter. It was a Frankenstein's monster of a season in reverse, or what would happen if an artist put out a *Worst Of...* record. The strikeout numbers from his walks-and-dingers years paired up with the walks and contact quality from his no-strikeout, no-power years. The only thing that didn't decline was Carpenter's salsa-making prowess, which is apparently still 80-grade. Until baseball starts awarding runs for perfectly-balanced mixes of flavor and spice, though, his contributions in the kitchen can't offset his on-field decline. Hopefully Carpenter has a jar of hard contact stored in a cabinet somewhere, because home runs are what will keep him in tomato money heading forward, even if that wasn't the case in 2019.

YEAR	TEAM	LVL	AGE	PA	DRC+	VORP	BABIP	BRR	FRAA	WARP
2017	SLN	MLB	31	622	119	34.8	.274	-2.4	1B(120): 2.1, 3B(16): 0.9	2.7
2018	SLN	MLB	32	677	135	55.6	.291	-1.5	1B(95): -3.6, 3B(76): 4.8	4.6
2019	SLN	MLB	33	492	96	15.9	.285	-1.9	3B(107): -6.5, 1B(4): -0.2	0.7
2020	SLN	MLB	34	469	104	12.4	.283	-1.6	3B 0, 1B 0	1.3

Matt Carpenter, continued

Batted Ball Distribution

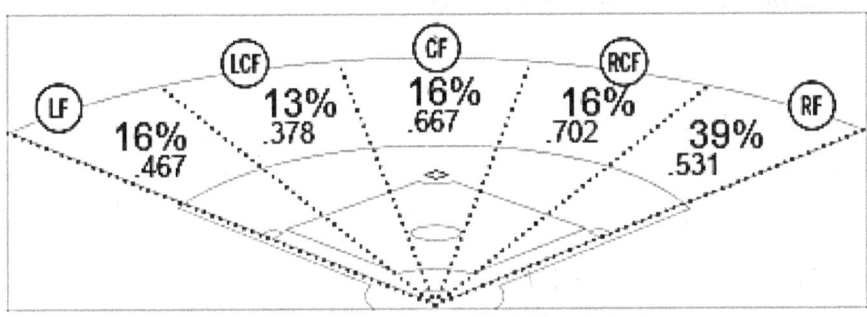

Strike Zone vs LHP **Strike Zone vs RHP**

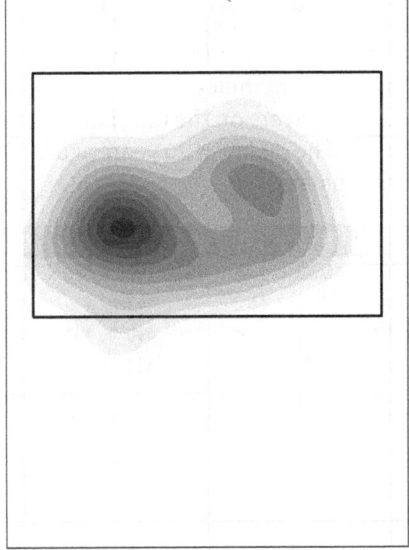

Paul DeJong SS

Born: 08/02/93 Age: 26 Bats: R Throws: R
Height: 6'0" Weight: 200 Origin: Round 4, 2015 Draft (#131 overall)

YEAR	TEAM	LVL	AGE	PA	R	2B	3B	HR	RBI	BB	K	SB	CS	AVG/OBP/SLG
2017	MEM	AAA	23	190	27	9	0	13	34	9	46	0	2	.299/.339/.571
2017	SLN	MLB	23	443	55	26	1	25	65	21	124	1	0	.285/.325/.532
2018	SLN	MLB	24	490	68	25	1	19	68	36	123	1	1	.241/.313/.433
2019	SLN	MLB	25	664	97	31	1	30	78	62	149	9	5	.233/.318/.444
2020	SLN	MLB	26	595	69	26	1	26	80	46	139	4	2	.230/.303/.430

Comparables: Trevor Story, Matt Joyce, Brad Miller

Few players embody the trends of modern baseball more than DeJong. He has the kind of frame that traditionally screams infield corner, but advances in defensive positioning turned him into an above-average shortstop. His contact problems and low batting average would have left him shunned in prior eras, but his power and improving batting eye are enough to make him an above-average offensive player despite middling back-of-the-baseball-card stats. And he even signed that most modern of contracts—the pre-extension guaranteeing he'll be drastically underpaid for most of his career. People are often said to be the product of their environments. DeJong is the product of his era. He's one of the best players on the Cardinals, and he might never have even seen the majors if he'd played 20 years ago. Score one for modern player evaluation and development.

YEAR	TEAM	LVL	AGE	PA	DRC+	VORP	BABIP	BRR	FRAA	WARP
2017	MEM	AAA	23	190	126	18.2	.336	-1.0	SS(39): -3.8, 2B(5): 0.4	1.0
2017	SLN	MLB	23	443	115	33.3	.349	-3.9	SS(86): -0.3, 2B(20): -0.7	2.3
2018	SLN	MLB	24	490	101	35.2	.288	3.1	SS(114): 0.3	2.7
2019	SLN	MLB	25	664	104	35.4	.259	0.5	SS(157): 7.1	4.2
2020	SLN	MLB	26	595	95	19.0	.262	0.0	SS 2	2.1

Paul DeJong, continued

Batted Ball Distribution

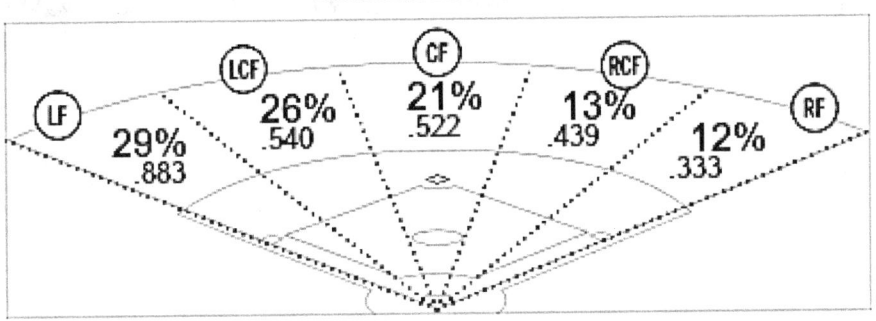

Strike Zone vs LHP   Strike Zone vs RHP

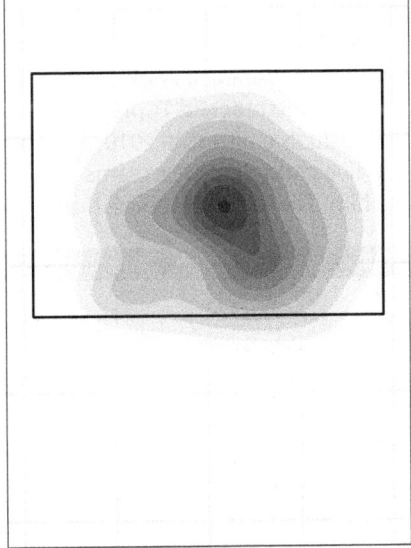

Tommy Edman INF

Born: 05/09/95 Age: 25 Bats: B Throws: R
Height: 5'10" Weight: 180 Origin: Round 6, 2016 Draft (#196 overall)

YEAR	TEAM	LVL	AGE	PA	R	2B	3B	HR	RBI	BB	K	SB	CS	AVG/OBP/SLG
2017	PEO	A	22	174	24	8	5	2	18	15	19	8	2	.284/.347/.439
2017	PMB	A+	22	82	7	2	1	1	11	7	18	0	1	.257/.338/.357
2017	SFD	AA	22	239	20	12	2	2	26	16	34	5	2	.247/.298/.347
2018	SFD	AA	23	498	71	23	3	6	36	35	76	27	5	.299/.350/.403
2018	MEM	AAA	23	76	13	0	1	1	5	8	11	3	0	.318/.382/.394
2019	MEM	AAA	24	218	39	12	4	7	29	15	33	9	0	.305/.356/.513
2019	SLN	MLB	24	349	59	17	7	11	36	16	61	15	1	.304/.350/.500
2020	SLN	MLB	25	595	59	25	7	14	64	33	109	13	4	.257/.306/.401

Comparables: Greg Litton, Johan Camargo, Ed Brinkman

Somewhere in the eldritch past, Cardinals fan Frederick Bird made a terrible bargain. He would forever be forced to inhabit the body of a giant plush bird, unable to talk but forced to interact with children every day. In exchange, Lucifer promised a little help with the farm system. We may never know whether Fredbird is happy with his infernal deal, but Edman is surely pleased to be the most recent beneficiary of the Devil Magic. How else could a diminutive middle infielder who reached Triple-A only in August 2018 become one of the lineup's most valuable hitters in 2019? He'll probably be an under-appreciated cog in the next five good Cardinals teams before passing the baton to someone vaguely like him. Thanks to Fredbird, that's just how it works at this point.

YEAR	TEAM	LVL	AGE	PA	DRC+	VORP	BABIP	BRR	FRAA	WARP
2017	PEO	A	22	174	126	16.0	.309	2.1	SS(38): -0.6	1.4
2017	PMB	A+	22	82	106	5.3	.327	-0.2	SS(15): -0.6, 2B(3): 0.1	0.3
2017	SFD	AA	22	239	77	4.3	.281	0.7	SS(61): 1.0	0.7
2018	SFD	AA	23	498	114	29.6	.345	3.4	SS(65): -1.4, 3B(22): 0.7	3.0
2018	MEM	AAA	23	76	119	7.8	.357	1.0	2B(14): 1.4, SS(3): -0.1	0.7
2019	MEM	AAA	24	218	102	19.1	.333	3.7	2B(25): 0.0, SS(10): -1.5	1.1
2019	SLN	MLB	24	349	110	16.8	.346	4.7	3B(55): 0.3, 2B(29): 0.7	2.3
2020	SLN	MLB	25	595	87	9.1	.297	3.2	3B 1, LF 0	1.2

Tommy Edman, continued

Batted Ball Distribution

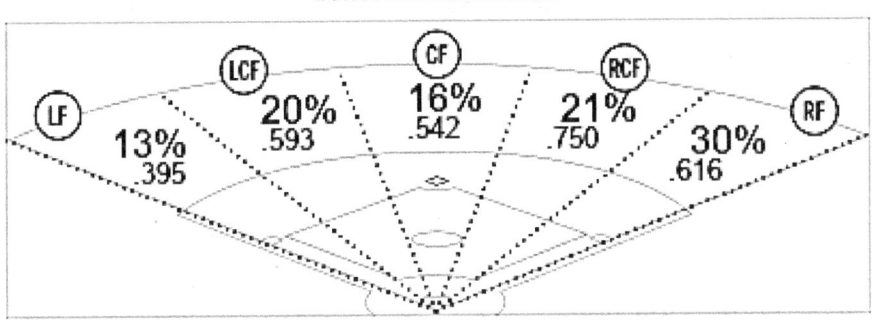

| Strike Zone vs LHP | Strike Zone vs RHP |

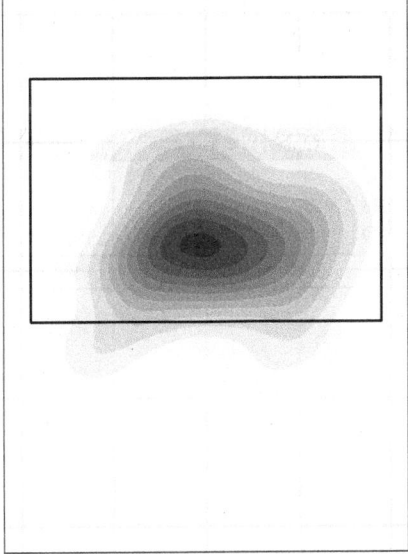

St. Louis Cardinals 2020

Dexter Fowler   RF
Born: 03/22/86   Age: 34   Bats: B   Throws: R
Height: 6'5"   Weight: 195   Origin: Round 14, 2004 Draft (#410 overall)

YEAR	TEAM	LVL	AGE	PA	R	2B	3B	HR	RBI	BB	K	SB	CS	AVG/OBP/SLG
2017	SLN	MLB	31	491	68	22	9	18	64	63	101	7	3	.264/.363/.488
2018	SLN	MLB	32	334	40	10	0	8	31	38	75	5	2	.180/.278/.298
2019	SLN	MLB	33	574	69	24	1	19	67	74	142	8	5	.238/.346/.409
2020	SLN	MLB	34	532	61	21	3	16	61	69	136	11	4	.232/.341/.398

Comparables: Curtis Granderson, Peter Bourjos, B.J. Upton

After a down 2018 in which pretty much everything went wrong, perhaps no player in baseball was more in need of a bounceback than Fowler. He won't consider 2019 an unqualified success, but the results were encouraging: nearly two wins of improvement, an extended stay at the leadoff spot in the Cardinals lineup, much-improved defense, and the second-most plate appearances of his career. He's not likely to get better from here—34-year-old outfielders are hardly a good bet to improve in the modern game—but he's surely thrilled to have gone from pariah to useful contributor to a playoff team. The Cardinals have young outfielders coming, but Fowler doesn't look like he's ready to surrender his spot just yet.

YEAR	TEAM	LVL	AGE	PA	DRC+	VORP	BABIP	BRR	FRAA	WARP
2017	SLN	MLB	31	491	118	37.8	.305	1.4	CF(109): -10.1	2.0
2018	SLN	MLB	32	334	77	-1.4	.210	2.0	RF(75): -4.3	-0.4
2019	SLN	MLB	33	574	100	16.4	.294	-0.5	RF(118): -0.3, CF(58): -3.4	1.2
2020	SLN	MLB	34	532	99	14.5	.296	1.0	RF 0, CF -2	1.2

Dexter Fowler, continued

Batted Ball Distribution

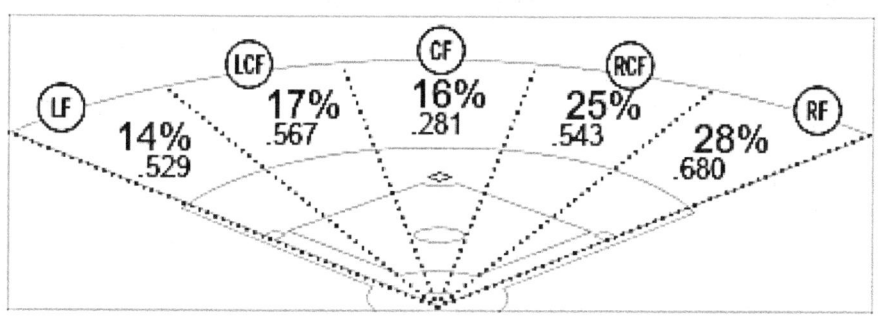

Strike Zone vs LHP   Strike Zone vs RHP

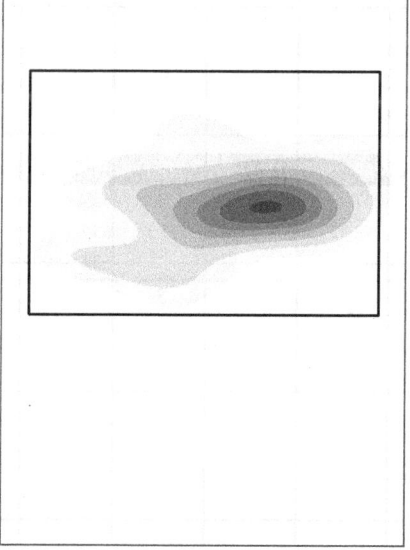

St. Louis Cardinals 2020

Paul Goldschmidt 1B

Born: 09/10/87 Age: 32 Bats: R Throws: R
Height: 6'3" Weight: 225 Origin: Round 8, 2009 Draft (#246 overall)

YEAR	TEAM	LVL	AGE	PA	R	2B	3B	HR	RBI	BB	K	SB	CS	AVG/OBP/SLG
2017	ARI	MLB	29	665	117	34	3	36	120	94	147	18	5	.297/.404/.563
2018	ARI	MLB	30	690	95	35	5	33	83	90	173	7	4	.290/.389/.533
2019	SLN	MLB	31	682	97	25	1	34	97	78	166	3	1	.260/.346/.476
2020	SLN	MLB	32	630	85	27	2	29	89	82	160	14	4	.264/.364/.478

Comparables: Pat Burrell, Travis Hafner, Jonny Gomes

If you're looking for a silver lining in Goldschmidt's down 2019, there are plenty of places you could start. You could look at his plate-discipline numbers and say everything looks normal. You could look at his second-half numbers and say that after the break, Goldschmidt was almost back to his old self. You could look at his defensive prowess, which the team raves about, as a hard-to-quantify boost to St. Louis's excellent defense. But the truth is, those are just silver linings. The stormcloud that was 2019 is scary. Maybe it was fluky, and maybe he'll be as good as ever in 2020, but aging curves aren't always smooth declines from excellence to mediocrity. Sometimes decline comes fast and never reverses. That's not the most likely outcome, but the fact that it's even a question now tells you how haywire things went in 2019.

YEAR	TEAM	LVL	AGE	PA	DRC+	VORP	BABIP	BRR	FRAA	WARP
2017	ARI	MLB	29	665	140	57.2	.343	3.7	1B(151): 5.7	5.1
2018	ARI	MLB	30	690	136	55.4	.359	-1.3	1B(155): 1.7	4.1
2019	SLN	MLB	31	682	119	27.9	.303	-0.8	1B(159): -7.3	1.9
2020	SLN	MLB	32	630	126	34.0	.323	0.4	1B 1	3.6

Paul Goldschmidt, *continued*

Batted Ball Distribution

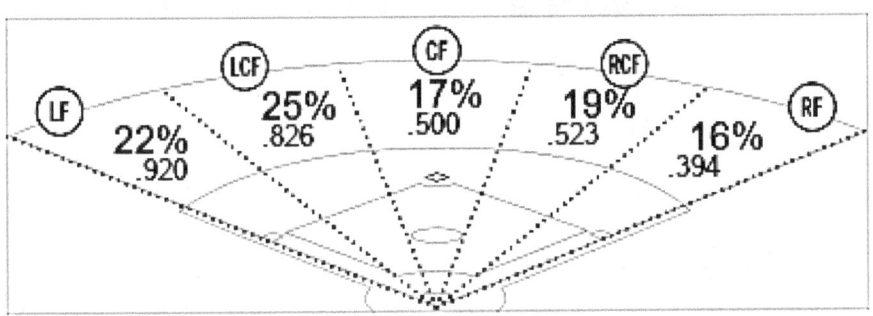

Strike Zone vs LHP   **Strike Zone vs RHP**

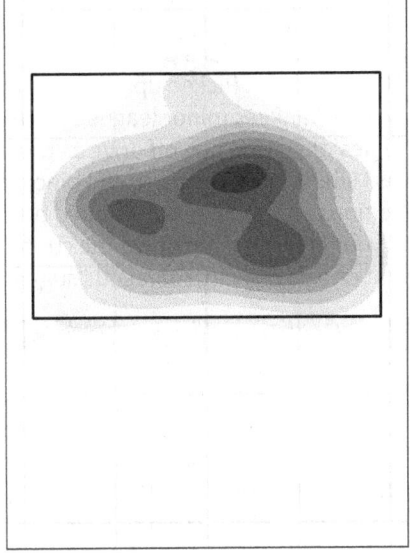

St. Louis Cardinals 2020

Brad Miller UT

Born: 10/18/89 Age: 30 Bats: L Throws: R
Height: 6'2" Weight: 215 Origin: Round 2, 2011 Draft (#62 overall)

YEAR	TEAM	LVL	AGE	PA	R	2B	3B	HR	RBI	BB	K	SB	CS	AVG/OBP/SLG
2017	TBA	MLB	27	407	43	13	3	9	40	63	110	5	3	.201/.327/.337
2018	CSP	AAA	28	31	4	0	0	1	2	3	9	1	0	.185/.258/.296
2018	TBA	MLB	28	174	16	10	1	5	21	16	51	0	0	.256/.322/.429
2018	MIL	MLB	28	80	5	3	1	2	8	6	31	0	0	.230/.288/.378
2019	SWB	AAA	29	163	31	9	1	10	29	24	40	1	3	.294/.399/.596
2019	PHI	MLB	29	130	22	3	1	12	21	11	35	1	0	.263/.331/.610
2019	CLE	MLB	29	40	4	3	0	1	4	4	10	1	0	.250/.325/.417
2020	PHI	MLB	30	251	30	10	1	11	34	26	69	3	1	.232/.314/.440

Comparables: Chris Taylor, Tom Tresh, Dick McAuliffe

Finding something symbolic of the 2019 Phillies' futility isn't hard, but perhaps nothing was more fitting than Miller's two-homer, four-RBI outburst on September 24. Not only had they been eliminated from the playoffs earlier that day after losing the first game of a doubleheader against the streaking Nationals, but Miller's performance couldn't even net them a meaningless win in the night cap. Picked up off the scrap heap after Philadelphia purchased him from the Yankees minor league system in June, Miller became a vital piece of the Phillies' thwarted playoff drive as the team around him collapsed. None of this was Miller's fault. He is a useful piece, a versatile player who can cover multiple positions and provide left-handed pop off the bench. However, if he's starting for your favorite team down the stretch, you've got a big problem regardless of what one day's worth of results suggested.

YEAR	TEAM	LVL	AGE	PA	DRC+	VORP	BABIP	BRR	FRAA	WARP
2017	TBA	MLB	27	407	84	7.8	.265	-1.3	2B(98): -1.3	0.1
2018	CSP	AAA	28	31	52	-2.2	.222	-0.7	SS(6): 0.2, 2B(1): 0.1	-0.1
2018	TBA	MLB	28	174	81	4.6	.343	-0.6	1B(35): -2.1, 2B(6): 0.2	-0.4
2018	MIL	MLB	28	80	83	-1.0	.366	-0.7	2B(15): 0.1, SS(6): -0.4	0.0
2019	SWB	AAA	29	163	133	14.9	.341	-0.7	2B(13): -0.9, LF(11): 0.6	0.8
2019	PHI	MLB	29	130	128	9.1	.268	0.3	3B(19): 0.4, LF(16): 1.3	1.1
2019	CLE	MLB	29	40	82	0.4	.320	0.7	2B(13): 0.4	0.1
2020	PHI	MLB	30	251	97	6.7	.282	-0.4	2B -1, 1B 0	0.6

Brad Miller, continued

Batted Ball Distribution

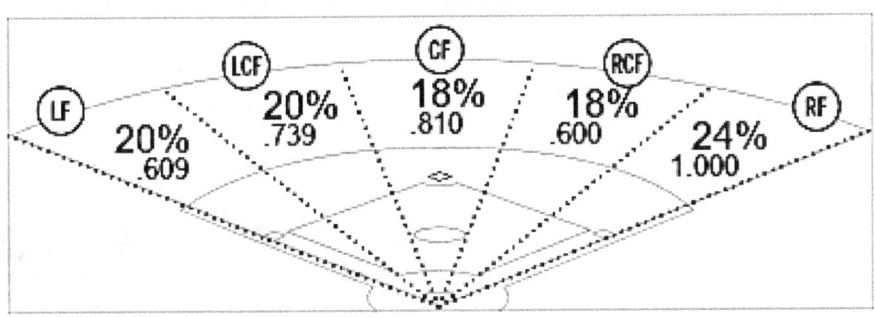

Strike Zone vs LHP   **Strike Zone vs RHP**

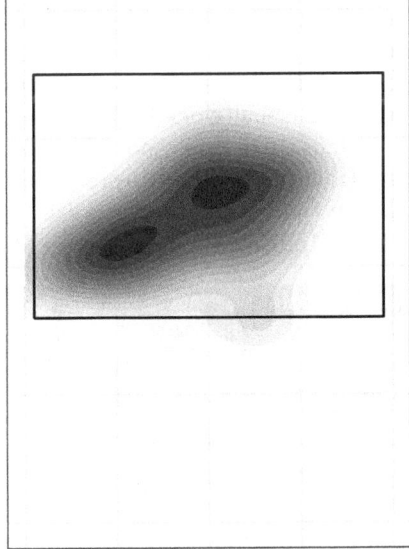

St. Louis Cardinals 2020

Yadier Molina C
Born: 07/13/82   Age: 37   Bats: R   Throws: R
Height: 5'11"   Weight: 205   Origin: Round 4, 2000 Draft (#113 overall)

YEAR	TEAM	LVL	AGE	PA	R	2B	3B	HR	RBI	BB	K	SB	CS	AVG/OBP/SLG
2017	SLN	MLB	34	543	60	27	1	18	82	28	74	9	4	.273/.312/.439
2018	SLN	MLB	35	503	55	20	0	20	74	29	66	4	3	.261/.314/.436
2019	SLN	MLB	36	452	45	24	0	10	57	23	58	6	0	.270/.312/.399
2020	SLN	MLB	37	525	51	26	1	13	57	28	83	5	2	.257/.305/.392

Comparables: Jason Kendall, Russ Nixon, Tony Peña

The year is 2063. Baseball franchises are worth more than ever despite average game length eclipsing four hours. Player salaries have remained stagnant since the Great Alex Rodríguez Riots of 2037. Baseball is still investigating whether the

YEAR	TEAM	P. COUNT	FRM RUNS	BLK RUNS	THRW RUNS	TOT RUNS
2017	SLN	18649	6.4	0.2	2.2	9.3
2018	SLN	17163	2.3	1.2	0.1	3.5
2019	SLN	15641	0.3	1.5	-0.1	1.5
2020	SLN	24468	6.2	0.4	-0.2	6.3

manufacturing process affects the aerodynamics of baseballs, an inquiry that peaked in urgency in 2035 when a 40-year-old Cody Bellinger hit 122 home runs (17 of which came on bunts). An automated strike-zone never took hold; instead, baseball cloned Joe West and Ángel Hernández to create a consistently ridiculous strike zone. And through it all, Molina has been catching 140 games a year for the Cardinals. Top prospect Andrew Knizner III, grandson of longtime backup Andrew Knizner, looks like a good bet to succeed Molina when he retires. (The day will never come, but don't tell Knizner that.)

YEAR	TEAM	LVL	AGE	PA	DRC+	VORP	BABIP	BRR	FRAA	WARP
2017	SLN	MLB	34	543	102	21.3	.285	-4.5	C(133): 6.0, 1B(1): 0.0	3.0
2018	SLN	MLB	35	503	111	28.1	.264	-2.3	C(121): 1.4, 1B(5): 0.0	3.1
2019	SLN	MLB	36	452	92	19.0	.289	-2.4	C(111): 0.6, 1B(4): 0.0	1.7
2020	SLN	MLB	37	525	85	11.4	.287	-2.8	C 5	1.6

Yadier Molina, continued

Batted Ball Distribution

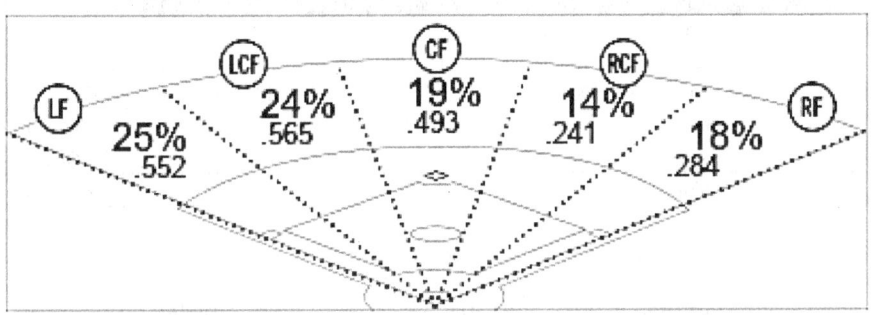

Strike Zone vs LHP

Strike Zone vs RHP

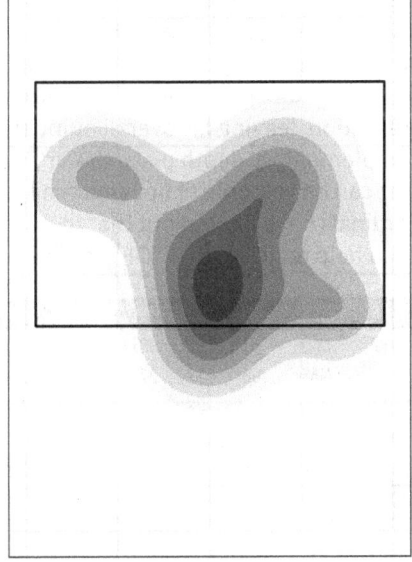

St. Louis Cardinals 2020

Yairo Muñoz INF

Born: 01/23/95   Age: 25   Bats: R   Throws: R
Height: 6'1"   Weight: 201   Origin: International Free Agent, 2012

YEAR	TEAM	LVL	AGE	PA	R	2B	3B	HR	RBI	BB	K	SB	CS	AVG/OBP/SLG
2017	MID	AA	22	207	35	17	3	6	26	10	35	12	1	.316/.348/.532
2017	NAS	AAA	22	272	30	9	1	7	42	11	46	10	4	.289/.316/.414
2018	MEM	AAA	23	100	11	3	1	3	13	5	18	1	0	.287/.330/.436
2018	SLN	MLB	23	329	39	16	0	8	42	30	71	5	6	.276/.350/.413
2019	SLN	MLB	24	181	20	7	1	2	13	7	37	8	3	.267/.298/.355
2020	SLN	MLB	25	161	16	8	1	4	17	9	35	2	1	.249/.294/.388

Comparables: Jorge Polanco, Eduardo Escobar, Didi Gregorius

When Muñoz debuted in 2018, the Citi Field scoreboard misspelled his name as "Yario." It was an honest mistake (or perhaps an homage to Mario's lesser-known nemesis?), but one that served as a harbinger for things to come. A quintessential utility infielder, Muñoz spent most of 2019 as out of position as the vowels in his name. For the first (and perhaps the last) time in his career, he saw considerable action in the outfield. Although his bat has never been outstanding, he hits lefties well enough to profile as either a spare infielder or the weak side of a platoon. The Cardinals haven't yet adhered to that evaluation, leaving his overall numbers to suffer as a result. Muñoz is the kind of complementary depth piece that most teams could find room for, and the kind that can be valuable (if not voluminous) with proper management. So far, the Cardinals have figured out that the "i" comes before the "r" in Yairo, they just need help realizing that "OF" should never come after "Muñoz."

YEAR	TEAM	LVL	AGE	PA	DRC+	VORP	BABIP	BRR	FRAA	WARP
2017	MID	AA	22	207	120	19.0	.355	3:2	SS(22): -1.1, 3B(21): -0.3	1.3
2017	NAS	AAA	22	272	92	7.7	.324	-2.9	SS(24): 2.4, CF(19): -1.9	0.7
2018	MEM	AAA	23	100	104	7.2	.329	0.3	SS(13): 0.2, LF(4): -0.5	0.3
2018	SLN	MLB	23	329	101	17.2	.338	-2.5	SS(40): -5.4, 2B(26): -0.8	0.2
2019	SLN	MLB	24	181	73	0.3	.328	0.8	3B(21): -0.1, SS(17): 0.1	0.0
2020	SLN	MLB	25	161	82	1.5	.298	-0.1	2B 0, SS 0	0.1

Yairo Muñoz, continued

Batted Ball Distribution

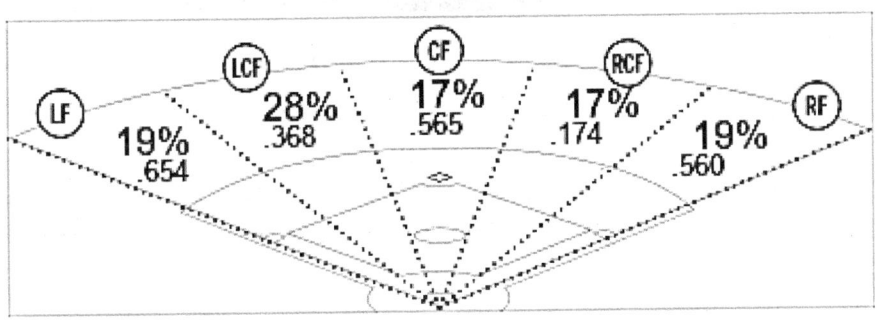

Strike Zone vs LHP   **Strike Zone vs RHP**

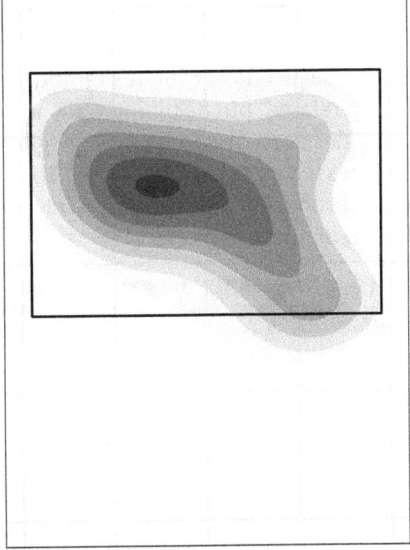

St. Louis Cardinals 2020

Tyler O'Neill LF

Born: 06/22/95   Age: 25   Bats: R   Throws: R
Height: 5'11"   Weight: 210   Origin: Round 3, 2013 Draft (#85 overall)

YEAR	TEAM	LVL	AGE	PA	R	2B	3B	HR	RBI	BB	K	SB	CS	AVG/OBP/SLG
2017	TAC	AAA	22	396	54	21	2	19	56	44	108	9	2	.244/.328/.479
2017	MEM	AAA	22	161	23	5	1	12	39	10	43	5	0	.253/.304/.548
2018	MEM	AAA	23	273	61	9	2	26	63	29	68	3	1	.311/.385/.693
2018	SLN	MLB	23	142	29	5	0	9	23	7	57	2	0	.254/.303/.500
2019	MEM	AAA	24	166	26	5	0	11	26	14	51	3	0	.265/.325/.517
2019	SLN	MLB	24	151	18	6	0	5	16	10	53	1	0	.262/.311/.411
2020	SLN	MLB	25	301	36	13	1	14	41	23	110	4	1	.234/.299/.439

Comparables: Randal Grichuk, Clint Frazier, Matt Olson

It's a shame O'Neill is from Canada, because he's Texas personified: everything is bigger with O'Neill. The muscles, the speed, the power—the strikeouts, and the attrition risk. O'Neill's profile has always been extreme, and he did nothing to change that in 2019, as he struck out more than 30 percent of the time in both Triple-A and the majors. Those sky-high numbers would be the end for many players, but O'Neill theoretically has the power to make the overall package work—he just hasn't yet. It's tempting to shrug off his struggles last season as injury-related, but declining walk numbers and general plate-discipline struggles are a discouraging sign, given his batting average is always going to be suppressed by his contact woes. The Cardinals' pipeline includes a number of other promising outfielders, so O'Neill needs to start proving his stuff before he's sent out to pasture.

YEAR	TEAM	LVL	AGE	PA	DRC+	VORP	BABIP	BRR	FRAA	WARP
2017	TAC	AAA	22	396	98	20.5	.295	0.3	LF(67): -1.8, RF(17): -0.9	0.6
2017	MEM	AAA	22	161	104	7.1	.266	-0.6	RF(18): 1.0, LF(10): -0.3	0.8
2018	MEM	AAA	23	273	159	40.8	.324	1.0	LF(33): -1.3, RF(21): 7.8	3.3
2018	SLN	MLB	23	142	90	11.6	.364	2.2	RF(24): 0.7, LF(16): 1.1	0.5
2019	MEM	AAA	24	166	104	10.8	.322	0.7	LF(25): 0.2, RF(11): 1.0	0.6
2019	SLN	MLB	24	151	75	-0.5	.386	-0.9	LF(33): -3.3, RF(8): -0.2	-0.4
2020	SLN	MLB	25	301	97	7.7	.332	0.5	LF -4	0.4

Tyler O'Neill, continued

Batted Ball Distribution

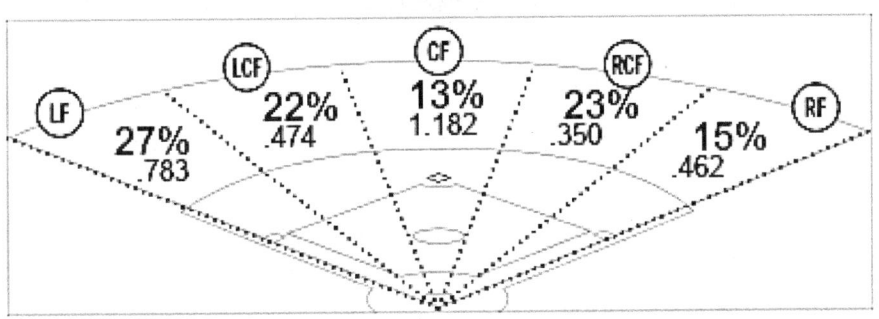

| Strike Zone vs LHP | Strike Zone vs RHP |

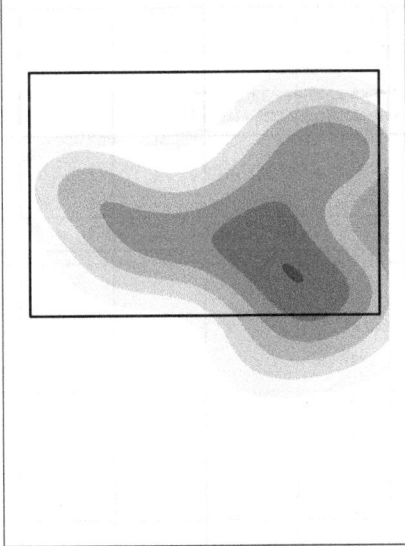

Matt Wieters C

Born: 05/21/86 Age: 34 Bats: B Throws: R
Height: 6'5" Weight: 235 Origin: Round 1, 2007 Draft (#5 overall)

YEAR	TEAM	LVL	AGE	PA	R	2B	3B	HR	RBI	BB	K	SB	CS	AVG/OBP/SLG
2017	WAS	MLB	31	465	43	20	0	10	52	38	94	1	0	.225/.288/.344
2018	WAS	MLB	32	271	24	8	0	8	30	30	45	0	1	.238/.330/.374
2019	SLN	MLB	33	183	15	4	0	11	27	12	47	1	1	.214/.268/.435
2020	SLN	MLB	34	251	27	11	0	9	31	20	61	1	0	.232/.297/.404

Comparables: Jason Varitek, John Buck, Ryan Doumit

Wieters completed the transition from underqualified starter to adequately qualified backup last season. His framing was quite poor—his large frame has always been identified as part of the reason why—but he's a well-regarded veteran who can run into a mistake now and then. He'll probably keep getting jobs, even if he's a threat to finish below replacement level from here on out.

YEAR	TEAM	P. COUNT	FRM RUNS	BLK RUNS	THRW RUNS	TOT RUNS
2017	WAS	16476	-11.2	1.5	-0.7	-11.0
2018	WAS	9086	-3.7	1.1	0.3	-2.3
2019	SLN	6250	-8.7	1.2	0.3	-7.3
2020	SLN	12894	-8.1	0.5	1.0	-6.7

YEAR	TEAM	LVL	AGE	PA	DRC+	VORP	BABIP	BRR	FRAA	WARP
2017	WAS	MLB	31	465	74	2.1	.264	-1.7	C(118): -10.4	-0.4
2018	WAS	MLB	32	271	101	8.1	.261	-0.8	C(73): -4.0	0.9
2019	SLN	MLB	33	183	97	8.6	.223	-0.8	C(54): -7.4	0.0
2020	SLN	MLB	34	251	84	2.3	.276	-0.6	C -7	-0.5

Matt Wieters, continued

Batted Ball Distribution

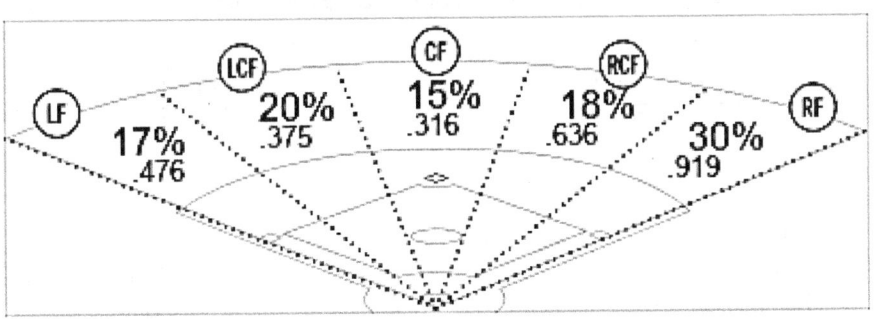

Strike Zone vs LHP

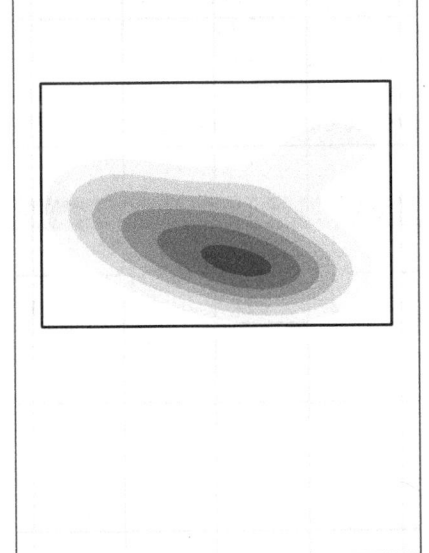

Strike Zone vs RHP

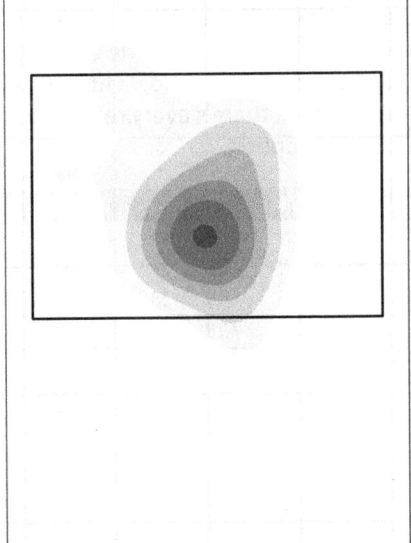

Kolten Wong 2B

Born: 10/10/90   Age: 29   Bats: L   Throws: R
Height: 5'9"   Weight: 185   Origin: Round 1, 2011 Draft (#22 overall)

YEAR	TEAM	LVL	AGE	PA	R	2B	3B	HR	RBI	BB	K	SB	CS	AVG/OBP/SLG
2017	SLN	MLB	26	411	55	27	3	4	42	41	60	8	2	.285/.376/.412
2018	SLN	MLB	27	407	41	18	2	9	38	31	60	6	5	.249/.332/.388
2019	SLN	MLB	28	549	61	25	4	11	59	47	83	24	4	.285/.361/.423
2020	SLN	MLB	29	595	62	27	4	13	62	48	100	12	4	.260/.337/.396

Comparables: Gordon Beckham, Bernie Allen, Cass Michaels

For as long as he's been in the majors, Wong has gone through stretches where he approaches stardom. He's been a great defender, shown sneaky power, reached base at an excellent clip, and provided value on the basepaths—just never all at the same time. In 2019, every thread came together to form his best season by far. You can't predict that for Wong going forward, of course, but his performance emphasizes his high floor. He strikes out less than average, walks (and gets hit by pitches) more than average, and plays excellent defense at second base. Those skills have always been there, which means he's roughly an average player even if some things go wrong, and a star-level performer when most things go right. Now entering the final season of the guaranteed portion of his contract, there's every reason to believe the Cardinals will be exercising their 2021 club option.

YEAR	TEAM	LVL	AGE	PA	DRC+	VORP	BABIP	BRR	FRAA	WARP
2017	SLN	MLB	26	411	97	23.9	.331	1.6	2B(106): -4.6	0.8
2018	SLN	MLB	27	407	91	11.8	.275	-2.0	2B(119): 6.0	1.2
2019	SLN	MLB	28	549	102	20.0	.321	3.2	2B(147): 18.6	4.1
2020	SLN	MLB	29	595	96	21.8	.299	0.6	2B 8	3.1

Kolten Wong, continued

Batted Ball Distribution

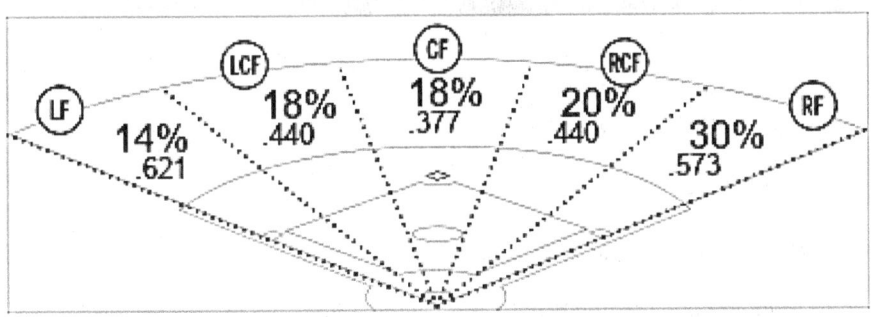

Strike Zone vs LHP   Strike Zone vs RHP

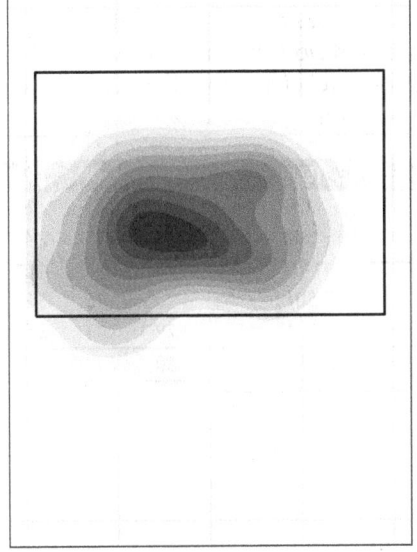

St. Louis Cardinals 2020

John Brebbia RHP

Born: 05/30/90 Age: 30 Bats: L Throws: R
Height: 6'1" Weight: 185 Origin: Round 30, 2011 Draft (#929 overall)

YEAR	TEAM	LVL	AGE	W	L	SV	G	GS	IP	H	HR	BB/9	K/9	K	GB%	BABIP
2017	MEM	AAA	27	1	1	3	15	1	26²	16	2	1.7	9.8	29	33%	.219
2017	SLN	MLB	27	0	0	0	50	0	51²	37	8	1.9	8.9	51	26%	.216
2018	MEM	AAA	28	2	0	2	11	0	13²	16	3	2.6	15.8	24	6%	.433
2018	SLN	MLB	28	3	3	2	45	0	50²	43	5	2.8	10.7	60	33%	.297
2019	SLN	MLB	29	3	4	0	66	0	72²	59	6	3.3	10.8	87	28%	.293
2020	SLN	MLB	30	3	3	0	58	0	61	51	9	2.7	10.3	70	28%	.276

Comparables: Erik Goeddel, Justin Grimm, Jacob Barnes

No one would have blamed Brebbia for calling it quits when the Yankees released him after the 2013 season. Instead, he spent two years in independent baseball, revamped his slider to better complement his fastball, and fought his way to the Show. Last season was his second year in a row of lights-out relief, and though the Cardinals still haven't used him in high-leverage roles very often, that's a reflection on the team's wide range of bullpen options rather than a lack of worthiness on his part. Brebbia will enter 2020 as an overqualified middle-relief arm, but if his career arc proves anything, it's that patience is often rewarded.

YEAR	TEAM	LVL	AGE	WHIP	ERA	DRA	WARP	MPH	FB%	WHF	CSP
2017	MEM	AAA	27	0.79	1.69	1.47	1.1				
2017	SLN	MLB	27	0.93	2.44	4.60	0.3	96.4	56.7	13.5	49.2
2018	MEM	AAA	28	1.46	4.61	3.60	0.2				
2018	SLN	MLB	28	1.16	3.20	2.92	1.2	97.1	53.3	13.8	49.8
2019	SLN	MLB	29	1.18	3.59	4.06	1.0	95.8	56.6	14.7	49.5
2020	SLN	MLB	30	1.12	3.25	3.68	1.2	95.5	55.5	14.1	49.4

John Brebbia, continued

Pitch Shape vs LHH

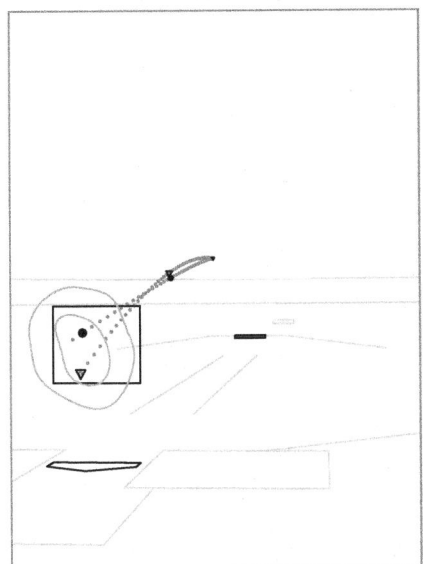

Pitch Shape vs RHH

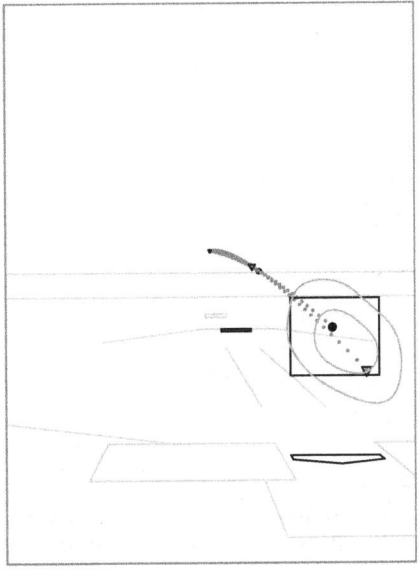

Type	Frequency	Velocity	H Movement	V Movement
● Fastball	56.6%	93.9 [104]	-7.5 [97]	-11.7 [111]
☐ Sinker				
+ Cutter				
▲ Changeup				
✕ Splitter				
▽ Slider	42.8%	84 [98]	7.3 [110]	-31.2 [105]
◇ Curveball				
⊕ Slow Curveball				
✻ Knuckleball				
▼ Screwball				

Génesis Cabrera LHP

Born: 10/10/96 Age: 23 Bats: L Throws: L
Height: 6'2" Weight: 190 Origin: International Free Agent, 2013

YEAR	TEAM	LVL	AGE	W	L	SV	G	GS	IP	H	HR	BB/9	K/9	K	GB%	BABIP
2017	PCH	A+	20	4	5	0	13	12	69^2	45	3	3.2	7.8	60	39%	.230
2017	MNT	AA	20	5	4	0	12	12	64^2	75	6	3.8	7.1	51	37%	.332
2018	MNT	AA	21	7	6	0	21	20	113^2	90	11	4.5	9.8	124	35%	.282
2018	SFD	AA	21	1	3	0	5	5	24^2	24	3	4.7	7.7	21	37%	.300
2019	MEM	AAA	22	5	6	0	20	18	99	107	20	3.5	9.6	106	42%	.330
2019	SLN	MLB	22	0	2	1	13	2	20^1	23	2	4.9	8.4	19	39%	.323
2020	SLN	MLB	23	3	4	0	38	6	63	65	10	3.8	7.1	49	38%	.295

Comparables: Eduardo Rodriguez, Jake Thompson, Lucas Giolito

In the beginning, the Cardinals had Tommy Pham. Then John Mozeliak said, let there be light. At first, the rest of the front office was confused, but he eventually revealed that he meant he wanted to trade Pham for a package including Cabrera. And so, here we are. Cabrera is a power-armed lefty who is still struggling to find a pitch to pair with his 96 mph heater. His changeup is the best of his secondaries, yet it features minimal velocity separation despite otherwise excellent deception. He started a full complement of games last year, but without a stronger breaker his version of Revelations is likely to include the bullpen.

YEAR	TEAM	LVL	AGE	WHIP	ERA	DRA	WARP	MPH	FB%	WHF	CSP
2017	PCH	A+	20	1.00	2.84	2.83	2.0				
2017	MNT	AA	20	1.58	3.62	5.63	-0.4				
2018	MNT	AA	21	1.29	4.12	4.27	1.4				
2018	SFD	AA	21	1.50	4.74	5.19	0.0				
2019	MEM	AAA	22	1.47	5.91	5.11	1.5				
2019	SLN	MLB	22	1.67	4.87	5.53	0.0	98.5	61	8.1	49.5
2020	SLN	MLB	23	1.46	4.85	5.02	0.4	98.4	63.2	8.4	51.3

Génesis Cabrera, continued

Pitch Shape vs LHH

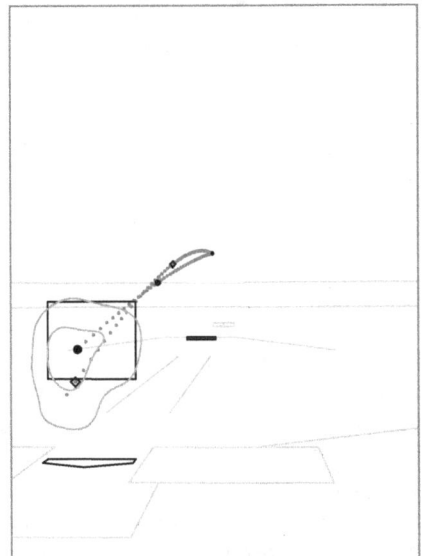

Pitch Shape vs RHH

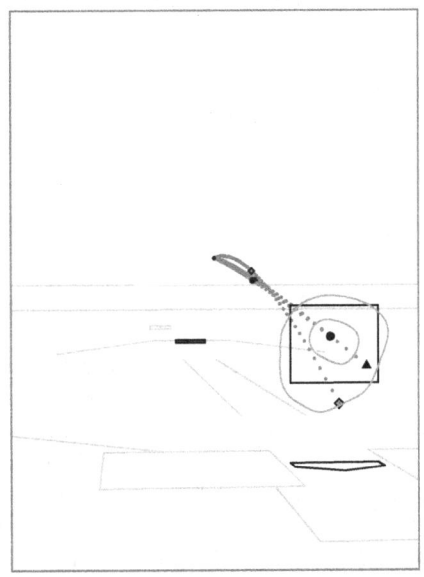

Type	Frequency	Velocity	H Movement	V Movement
● Fastball	56.5%	96.6 [112]	8.1 [95]	-11 [113]
☐ Sinker	4.6%	95.4 [115]	13.2 [97]	-14.8 [120]
+ Cutter				
▲ Changeup	17.5%	88.4 [111]	12 [96]	-20.5 [120]
✕ Splitter				
▽ Slider				
◇ Curveball	21.5%	82.9 [114]	-2.4 [80]	-44.9 [106]
⊕ Slow Curveball				
✳ Knuckleball				
▼ Screwball				

Junior Fernandez   RHP

Born: 03/02/97   Age: 23   Bats: R   Throws: R
Height: 6'1"   Weight: 180   Origin: International Free Agent, 2014

YEAR	TEAM	LVL	AGE	W	L	SV	G	GS	IP	H	HR	BB/9	K/9	K	GB%	BABIP
2017	PMB	A+	20	5	3	0	16	16	90¹	82	5	3.9	5.8	58	45%	.281
2018	PMB	A+	21	1	0	3	8	0	9²	9	0	1.9	6.5	7	43%	.321
2018	SFD	AA	21	0	0	0	16	0	21	19	1	6.9	7.3	17	36%	.295
2019	PMB	A+	22	0	0	4	9	0	11²	8	0	6.2	8.5	11	45%	.258
2019	SFD	AA	22	1	1	5	18	0	29	18	0	3.4	13.0	42	48%	.295
2019	MEM	AAA	22	2	1	2	18	0	24¹	17	0	4.1	10.0	27	63%	.274
2019	SLN	MLB	22	0	1	0	13	0	11²	9	2	4.6	12.3	16	50%	.269
2020	SLN	MLB	23	2	2	0	32	0	34	27	4	5.5	13.7	51	47%	.322

Comparables: Touki Toussaint, Jonathan Hernández, Tyrell Jenkins

The belief that every team could manufacture a good bullpen out of bubblegum and failed starters bouncing around the minors is tired. If it were that easy, there wouldn't be bad bullpens; there wouldn't be failed relief conversions. But, if you want to know why it's perpetually tempting, look no further than Fernandez. In 2017, he walked nearly as many batters as he struck out in A-ball. He was converted to relief thereafter, and he's since made it to the majors while posting an aggregate 2.52 ERA and striking out more than a quarter of opponents. Not all starters make excellent relievers; Fernandez might though.

YEAR	TEAM	LVL	AGE	WHIP	ERA	DRA	WARP	MPH	FB%	WHF	CSP
2017	PMB	A+	20	1.34	3.69	4.91	0.4				
2018	PMB	A+	21	1.14	0.00	4.69	0.0				
2018	SFD	AA	21	1.67	5.14	6.42	-0.4				
2019	PMB	A+	22	1.37	1.54	4.57	0.0				
2019	SFD	AA	22	1.00	1.55	3.03	0.6				
2019	MEM	AAA	22	1.15	1.48	2.36	0.9				
2019	SLN	MLB	22	1.29	5.40	3.34	0.3	99.0	41.7	19.7	39.7
2020	SLN	MLB	23	1.41	4.09	4.22	0.4	98.9	43.2	20.4	41.1

Junior Fernandez, continued

Pitch Shape vs LHH

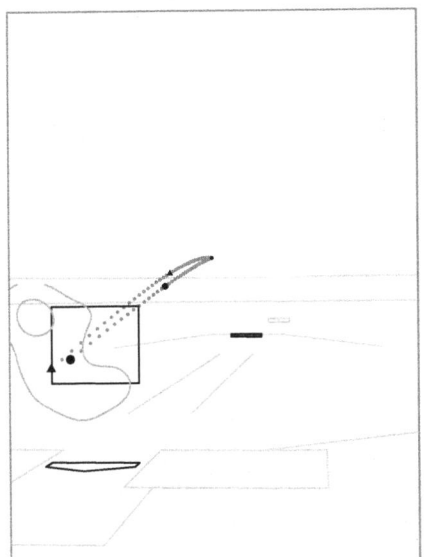

Pitch Shape vs RHH

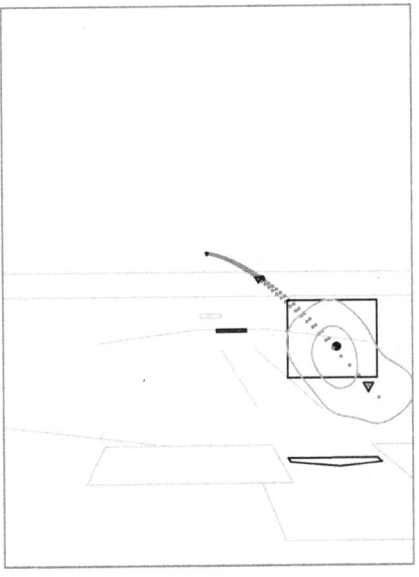

Type	Frequency	Velocity	H Movement	V Movement
● Fastball	41.7%	97 [113]	-10.5 [84]	-15.1 [102]
□ Sinker				
+ Cutter				
▲ Changeup	31.7%	86.3 [104]	-11.9 [97]	-29.2 [95]
× Splitter				
▽ Slider	26.6%	87 [111]	1.5 [85]	-27.4 [116]
◇ Curveball				
⊕ Slow Curveball				
✳ Knuckleball				
▼ Screwball				

St. Louis Cardinals 2020

Jack Flaherty   RHP
Born: 10/15/95   Age: 24   Bats: R   Throws: R
Height: 6'4"   Weight: 205   Origin: Round 1, 2014 Draft (#34 overall)

YEAR	TEAM	LVL	AGE	W	L	SV	G	GS	IP	H	HR	BB/9	K/9	K	GB%	BABIP
2017	SFD	AA	21	7	2	0	10	10	63^1	47	2	1.6	8.8	62	41%	.269
2017	MEM	AAA	21	7	2	0	15	15	85^1	73	10	2.5	9.0	85	42%	.288
2017	SLN	MLB	21	0	2	0	6	5	21^1	23	4	4.2	8.4	20	49%	.322
2018	MEM	AAA	22	4	1	0	5	5	31^2	22	2	2.0	11.7	41	44%	.274
2018	SLN	MLB	22	8	9	0	28	28	151	108	20	3.5	10.8	182	43%	.257
2019	SLN	MLB	23	11	8	0	33	33	196^1	135	25	2.5	10.6	231	41%	.242
2020	SLN	MLB	24	12	8	0	29	29	172	132	23	3.0	10.9	209	41%	.270

Comparables: Héctor Rondón, Yovani Gallardo, Luis Severino

It's generally quite hard to put yourself in a star athlete's shoes. They were the best kid in their class at every sport growing up, wunderkinds without equal, rarely failing at anything. Then they joined pro ball and outperformed older players at every turn. Stars arrive in the major leagues with a warped sense of reality—their world has always revolved around them, everyone else merely a prop in their play. But Flaherty doesn't quite fit this mold. Oh, he's a freak athlete, no doubt about that. But he pitched on the same high school team as Max Fried and Lucas Giolito, both of whom were first-round picks. Giolito was popping 100 mph as a prep, for crying out loud.

What could be more relatable than being excellent at a thing, only for someone at your school to outdo you? To call your friends to brag about your accomplishments, only to have them think "Lucas and Max did it better"—who among us hasn't told our parents what we accomplished this week, knowing that they're silently comparing us to that one person in our high school who was perfect? In a land populated mostly with unrelatable pillars of excellence, Flaherty represents a rare glimpse of humanity.

Of course, it's only a glimpse.

Flaherty is still very much unlike you. His career arc hasn't taken him the way most people go, leading a perfectly successful life that is nonetheless eclipsed by a frenemy. Instead of idling through life, content in his lot, he worked maniacally to get better. Instead of heading home after a day at work and sitting on the couch to watch TV, he started taking lessons in mound presence from Bob Gibson. While you got a "meets expectations" on your quarterly performance review, Flaherty posted a 0.91 ERA in the second half and crashed the Cy Young race, dragging the Cardinals into the playoffs in the process.

Just to emphasize the point, Flaherty won the series-deciding game against

Fried's Braves, and even drove in a run with Fried on the mound. He's the unquestioned best of that trio now, one of the 15 or so best starters in baseball. So while in some sense Flaherty is just like us, in another sense his story is even more inconceivable. The star athlete who was always the best is so different from you that it's easy to believe you could accomplish the same thing, were you in their shoes. Flaherty was in your shoes—and he *still* ended up on top. What could be more unrelatable than that?

YEAR	TEAM	LVL	AGE	WHIP	ERA	DRA	WARP	MPH	FB%	WHF	CSP
2017	SFD	AA	21	0.92	1.42	2.61	1.9				
2017	MEM	AAA	21	1.14	2.74	3.12	2.4				
2017	SLN	MLB	21	1.55	6.33	3.28	0.5	95.0	55.9	14	47.2
2018	MEM	AAA	22	0.92	2.27	2.07	1.2				
2018	SLN	MLB	22	1.11	3.34	3.07	3.9	95.9	55.3	14.5	46
2019	SLN	MLB	23	0.97	2.75	2.44	7.1	96.7	57.7	14.9	46.2
2020	*SLN*	*MLB*	*24*	*1.10*	*2.87*	*3.28*	*4.8*	*96.1*	*58.4*	*15.1*	*47.8*

Jack Flaherty, continued

Pitch Shape vs LHH

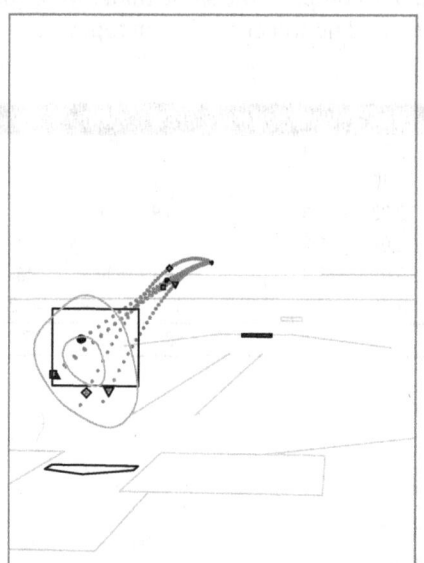

Pitch Shape vs RHH

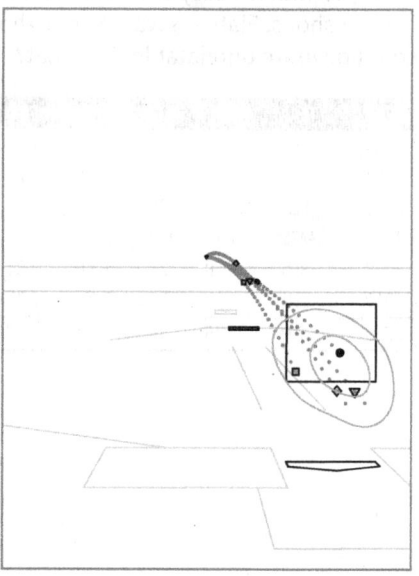

Type	Frequency	Velocity	H Movement	V Movement
● Fastball	46.1%	94.7 [106]	-4 [113]	-14.2 [104]
☐ Sinker	11.6%	92.5 [100]	-9.8 [118]	-21.1 [98]
+ Cutter				
▲ Changeup				
✕ Splitter				
▽ Slider	27.5%	85.1 [103]	6.1 [105]	-29.6 [110]
◇ Curveball	12.1%	78.5 [99]	11.9 [118]	-50.2 [94]
⊕ Slow Curveball				
✳ Knuckleball				
▼ Screwball				

Giovanny Gallegos RHP

Born: 08/14/91 Age: 28 Bats: R Throws: R
Height: 6'2" Weight: 210 Origin: International Free Agent, 2011

YEAR	TEAM	LVL	AGE	W	L	SV	G	GS	IP	H	HR	BB/9	K/9	K	GB%	BABIP
2017	SWB	AAA	25	4	2	5	28	0	43.1	28	4	2.3	14.3	69	32%	.286
2017	NYA	MLB	25	0	1	0	16	0	20.1	21	3	2.2	9.7	22	37%	.316
2018	SWB	AAA	26	2	1	2	17	0	27.2	24	1	2.3	13.3	41	39%	.354
2018	MEM	AAA	26	0	0	1	13	0	16.2	7	0	1.6	8.6	16	45%	.175
2018	NYA	MLB	26	0	0	1	4	0	10	10	2	2.7	9.0	10	41%	.320
2018	SLN	MLB	26	0	0	0	2	0	1.1	1	0	0.0	13.5	2	0%	.333
2019	SLN	MLB	27	3	2	1	66	0	74	44	9	1.9	11.3	93	34%	.222
2020	SLN	MLB	28	3	3	7	58	0	61	48	9	2.7	11.4	78	34%	.280

Comparables: Phil Maton, Jonathan Holder, Nick Wittgren

Believe it or not, Gallegos didn't start the year in the majors despite gaudy minor-league numbers. The Cardinals saw the light quickly enough, though, promoting Gallegos in April. From thereon, he accumulated more WARP than any other Cardinals reliever. His success wasn't startling—his minor-league strikeout and run-prevention numbers were excellent—but the timing was perfect for the Cardinals, whose patchwork starting rotation stacked a lot of pressure on a bullpen that had already lost Jordan Hicks earlier in the year. If he can keep it up, the Luke Voit trade—which was briefly known as the Chasen Shreve trade—might end up being remembered as the Giovanny Gallegos trade.

YEAR	TEAM	LVL	AGE	WHIP	ERA	DRA	WARP	MPH	FB%	WHF	CSP
2017	SWB	AAA	25	0.90	2.08	1.60	1.8				
2017	NYA	MLB	25	1.28	4.87	3.15	0.5	95.6	63.5	15.3	49.6
2018	SWB	AAA	26	1.12	3.90	2.95	0.7				
2018	MEM	AAA	26	0.60	0.54	1.85	0.6				
2018	NYA	MLB	26	1.30	4.50	5.38	-0.1	95.7	58.6	8.9	50.5
2018	SLN	MLB	26	0.75	0.00	6.81	0.0	96.3	64	12	46.2
2019	SLN	MLB	27	0.81	2.31	2.82	2.0	95.3	55.2	17.4	46.5
2020	SLN	MLB	28	1.08	2.92	3.34	1.4	94.8	57.2	16.4	48.7

St. Louis Cardinals 2020

Giovanny Gallegos, continued

Pitch Shape vs LHH

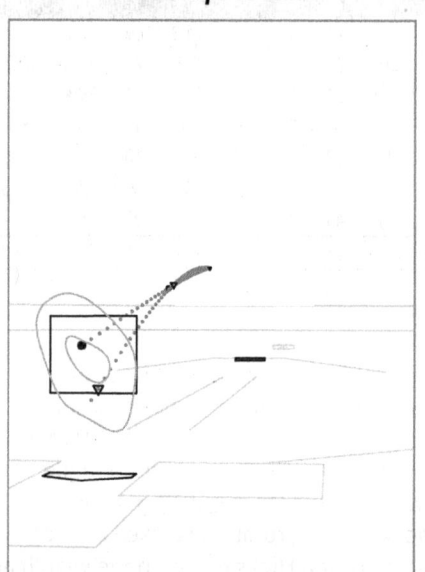

Pitch Shape vs RHH

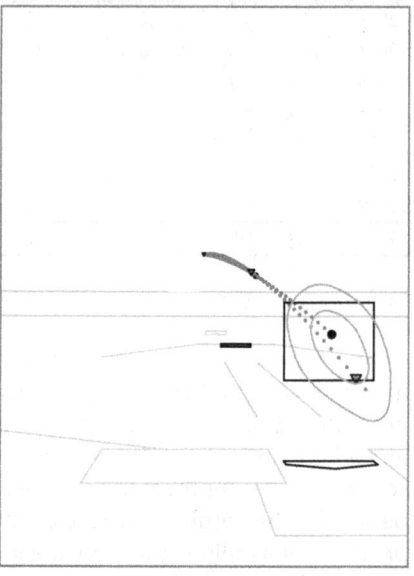

Type	Frequency	Velocity	H Movement	V Movement
● Fastball	55.2%	93.9 [104]	-9 [91]	-12.2 [110]
☐ Sinker				
+ Cutter				
▲ Changeup				
✕ Splitter				
▽ Slider	44.2%	85.5 [105]	0.8 [82]	-33.8 [98]
◇ Curveball				
⊕ Slow Curveball				
✳ Knuckleball				
▼ Screwball				

John Gant RHP

Born: 08/06/92 Age: 27 Bats: R Throws: R
Height: 6'3" Weight: 200 Origin: Round 21, 2011 Draft (#642 overall)

YEAR	TEAM	LVL	AGE	W	L	SV	G	GS	IP	H	HR	BB/9	K/9	K	GB%	BABIP
2017	MEM	AAA	24	6	5	0	18	18	103^1	109	10	2.2	8.6	99	47%	.334
2017	SLN	MLB	24	0	1	0	7	2	17^1	17	4	5.2	5.7	11	54%	.260
2018	MEM	AAA	25	5	1	0	8	8	49	45	5	2.9	7.7	42	49%	.288
2018	SLN	MLB	25	7	6	0	26	19	114	91	9	4.5	7.5	95	46%	.253
2019	SLN	MLB	26	11	1	3	64	0	66^1	51	4	4.6	8.1	60	46%	.275
2020	SLN	MLB	27	2	2	0	48	0	50	44	6	4.0	8.7	49	49%	.282

Comparables: Luis Cessa, Hunter Wood, Anthony Banda

It may feel weird to you that Gant didn't make the postseason roster; after all, he had an 11-1 record and a totally reasonable 3.66 ERA. Heck, even DRA liked his season well enough. What's not to love? Well, dig a little deeper, and it starts to get ugly. As the year wore on, his fastball velocity and command both dipped precipitously. How steep are we talking? In the first half of the season, he walked nine percent of the batters he faced. Over the subsequent months, that rate climbed to 11 percent, then 19 percent, then 29 percent in September (although, to be fair, that was against just 28 batters). Pretty much all of his other stats cratered as well, justifiably leaving him on the outside looking in. Here's hoping Gant can find a to avoid a similar trend in 2020.

YEAR	TEAM	LVL	AGE	WHIP	ERA	DRA	WARP	MPH	FB%	WHF	CSP
2017	MEM	AAA	24	1.30	3.83	4.06	1.9				
2017	SLN	MLB	24	1.56	4.67	5.03	0.1	95.8	65.2	11	46.1
2018	MEM	AAA	25	1.24	1.65	3.73	1.0				
2018	SLN	MLB	25	1.30	3.47	4.05	1.6	95.8	55.4	12.2	48.5
2019	SLN	MLB	26	1.28	3.66	4.32	0.7	98.0	55.7	13	48.4
2020	SLN	MLB	27	1.32	3.75	4.05	0.8	96.2	56.8	12.6	48.4

John Gant, continued

Pitch Shape vs LHH

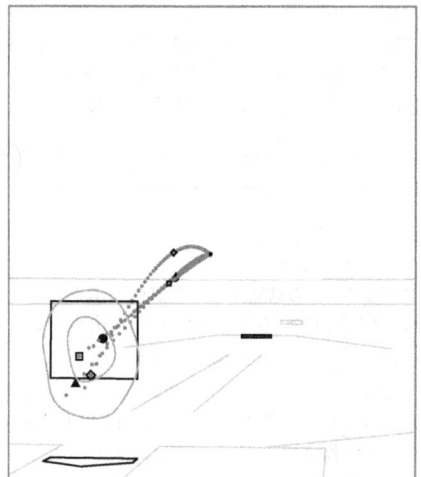

Pitch Shape vs RHH

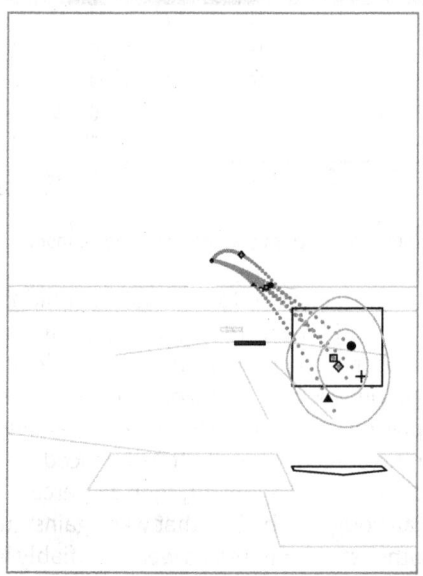

Type	Frequency	Velocity	H Movement	V Movement
● Fastball	25.4%	96.3 [111]	-9.8 [87]	-12.1 [110]
☐ Sinker	30.2%	96.2 [118]	-13.5 [95]	-15.3 [118]
+ Cutter	11.1%	90.6 [112]	2.2 [102]	-21.6 [109]
▲ Changeup	22.6%	83.4 [93]	-10.5 [103]	-29.2 [95]
✕ Splitter				
▽ Slider				
◇ Curveball	10.4%	77.5 [96]	7.5 [100]	-55.7 [83]
✦ Slow Curveball				
✱ Knuckleball				
▼ Screwball				

Ryan Helsley RHP

Born: 07/18/94 Age: 25 Bats: R Throws: R
Height: 6'1" Weight: 195 Origin: Round 5, 2015 Draft (#161 overall)

YEAR	TEAM	LVL	AGE	W	L	SV	G	GS	IP	H	HR	BB/9	K/9	K	GB%	BABIP
2017	PMB	A+	22	8	2	0	17	16	93^2	72	3	2.9	8.7	91	44%	.277
2017	SFD	AA	22	3	1	0	6	6	33^2	25	4	4.0	11.0	41	43%	.262
2018	SFD	AA	23	3	2	0	7	7	41	30	5	4.4	9.7	44	49%	.243
2018	MEM	AAA	23	2	1	0	5	5	26^2	18	2	3.0	11.5	34	38%	.262
2019	MEM	AAA	24	2	3	1	17	7	37^1	29	3	4.8	9.9	41	43%	.286
2019	SLN	MLB	24	2	0	0	24	0	36^2	34	5	2.9	7.9	32	35%	.279
2020	SLN	MLB	25	2	2	0	32	0	34	33	5	3.5	8.0	30	38%	.292

Comparables: Rafael Montero, Nestor Cortes Jr., Jakob Junis

If you didn't follow the Cardinals much in 2019, you might know Helsley only for his comments about how Atlanta's tomahawk chop chant devalues Native Americans. Brave is an overused adjective in sports, but it fits the bill here. No matter what he does the rest of his career, speaking up against a demeaning practice will define Helsley—there are few nobler things to be remembered for, in baseball or otherwise. This is purportedly a book about the game, so we'll note that he's a quality pitcher as well. His overpowering fastball and plus cutter and curve would look at home in the back of any bullpen, and it's possible the Cardinals are affording him the opportunity to win a rotation spot as you read this.

YEAR	TEAM	LVL	AGE	WHIP	ERA	DRA	WARP	MPH	FB%	WHF	CSP
2017	PMB	A+	22	1.09	2.69	3.40	2.0				
2017	SFD	AA	22	1.19	2.67	3.16	0.8				
2018	SFD	AA	23	1.22	4.39	3.52	0.9				
2018	MEM	AAA	23	1.01	3.71	2.63	0.9				
2019	MEM	AAA	24	1.31	4.58	3.09	1.2				
2019	SLN	MLB	24	1.25	2.95	5.04	0.1	100.2	56.6	11.3	51.7
2020	SLN	MLB	25	1.36	4.25	4.55	0.3	99.9	58	11.6	53

St. Louis Cardinals 2020

Ryan Helsley, continued

Pitch Shape vs LHH

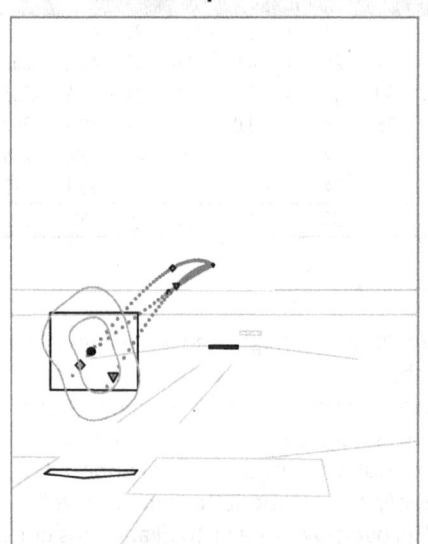

Pitch Shape vs RHH

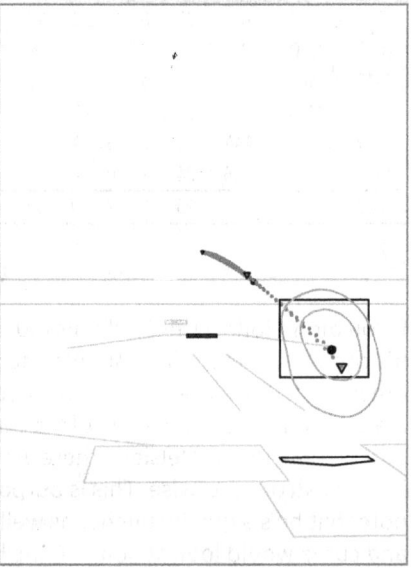

Type	Frequency	Velocity	H Movement	V Movement
● Fastball	56.6%	98 [116]	-6 [104]	-10.9 [113]
☐ Sinker				
+ Cutter				
▲ Changeup				
✕ Splitter				
▽ Slider	31.9%	89 [119]	4.2 [97]	-25.6 [121]
◇ Curveball	8.7%	81.1 [108]	1.3 [75]	-43.4 [109]
✦ Slow Curveball				
✱ Knuckleball				
▼ Screwball				

Jordan Hicks RHP

Born: 09/06/96 Age: 23 Bats: R Throws: R
Height: 6'2" Weight: 185 Origin: Round SUP, 2015 Draft (#105 overall)

YEAR	TEAM	LVL	AGE	W	L	SV	G	GS	IP	H	HR	BB/9	K/9	K	GB%	BABIP
2017	PEO	A	20	8	2	0	14	14	78	75	3	4.5	7.3	63	53%	.316
2017	PMB	A+	20	0	1	1	8	5	27	21	0	2.0	10.7	32	67%	.318
2018	SLN	MLB	21	3	4	6	73	0	77^2	59	2	5.2	8.1	70	62%	.266
2019	SLN	MLB	22	2	2	14	29	0	28^2	16	2	3.5	9.7	31	67%	.215
2020	SLN	MLB	23	1	1	0	11	0	11	10	1	5.2	10.4	13	62%	.319

Comparables: Clay Holmes, Jason García, Neil Ramírez

Hicks is best known for his blazing fastball, but he was developing into more than that before Tommy John surgery cut his season short. His slider, which averages around 87 mph and yet still sits 15 ticks below his heater, took a step forward and coerced whiffs on nearly 60 percent of the swings taken against it. He had also introduced a cromulent changeup to attack lefties. Those gains led him to post a better strikeout, walk, and groundball rate as compared to his rookie season. Hicks will likely return in the second half, and we can only hope he's as thrilling to watch as he was pre-injury.

YEAR	TEAM	LVL	AGE	WHIP	ERA	DRA	WARP	MPH	FB%	WHF	CSP
2017	PEO	A	20	1.46	3.35	5.50	-0.2				
2017	PMB	A+	20	1.00	1.00	3.58	0.5				
2018	SLN	MLB	21	1.34	3.59	6.03	-1.0	103.3	78	10.1	47.1
2019	SLN	MLB	22	0.94	3.14	3.22	0.7	103.9	60.3	12.7	46
2020	SLN	MLB	23	1.50	4.38	4.44	0.1	103.4	75.3	11.3	48.2

St. Louis Cardinals 2020

Jordan Hicks, continued

Pitch Shape vs LHH

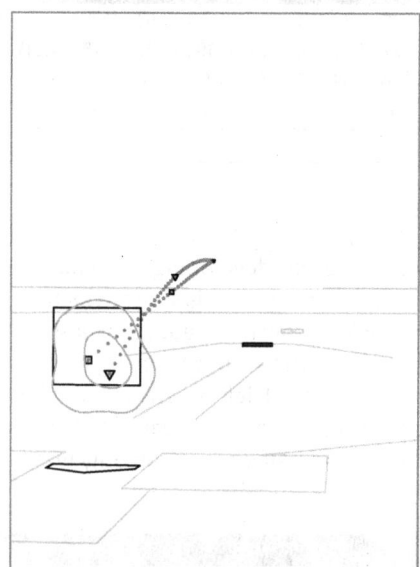

Pitch Shape vs RHH

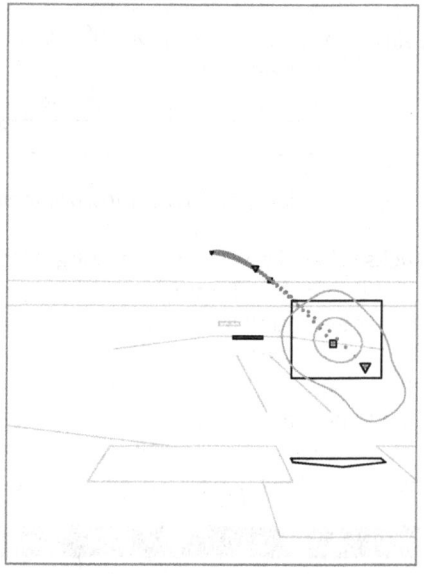

Type	Frequency	Velocity	H Movement	V Movement
● Fastball	3.4%	102.7 [129]	-11.6 [79]	-11.1 [113]
☐ Sinker	56.9%	101.6 [147]	-14 [92]	-15 [119]
+ Cutter				
▲ Changeup	3.9%	91.9 [124]	-7.4 [118]	-27.6 [99]
✕ Splitter				
▽ Slider	35.8%	87.5 [113]	8.8 [116]	-33.1 [100]
◇ Curveball				
⊕ Slow Curveball				
✱ Knuckleball				
▼ Screwball				

Dakota Hudson RHP

Born: 09/15/94 Age: 25 Bats: R Throws: R
Height: 6'5" Weight: 215 Origin: Round 1, 2016 Draft (#34 overall)

YEAR	TEAM	LVL	AGE	W	L	SV	G	GS	IP	H	HR	BB/9	K/9	K	GB%	BABIP
2017	SFD	AA	22	9	4	0	18	18	114	111	5	2.7	6.1	77	58%	.296
2017	MEM	AAA	22	1	1	0	7	7	38^2	36	2	3.5	4.4	19	59%	.272
2018	MEM	AAA	23	13	3	0	19	19	111^2	107	1	3.1	7.0	87	59%	.313
2018	SLN	MLB	23	4	1	0	26	0	27^1	19	0	5.9	6.3	19	64%	.237
2019	SLN	MLB	24	16	7	1	33	32	174^2	160	22	4.4	7.0	136	57%	.274
2020	SLN	MLB	25	9	9	0	26	26	143	137	17	3.9	7.2	114	57%	.286

Comparables: Jarred Cosart, Rob Whalen, Jake Odorizzi

Hudson is a glitch in the matrix—a groundball rate that must have been a transcription error, nearly as many walks as strikeouts, home runs on nearly 20 percent of his fly balls, easily exposed platoon issues against left-handed batters, and so on. Yet all that somehow adds up to a boring, slightly-better-than-average DRA? It all smacks of fiction. It's real life, though, and Hudson's particular brand of conflicting extremes works out to a serviceable starter, even if he doesn't get there in a normal way. Combine his worm-killing ways with the Cardinals' excellent infield defense, which makes his grounder-based game play up, and Hudson should again outperform his metrics as part of the rotation.

YEAR	TEAM	LVL	AGE	WHIP	ERA	DRA	WARP	MPH	FB%	WHF	CSP
2017	SFD	AA	22	1.27	2.53	4.47	0.9				
2017	MEM	AAA	22	1.32	4.42	3.47	0.9				
2018	MEM	AAA	23	1.30	2.50	3.63	2.4				
2018	SLN	MLB	23	1.35	2.63	6.41	-0.5	97.7	60.7	9.9	47.3
2019	SLN	MLB	24	1.41	3.35	4.49	2.4	95.6	61.7	10.4	46.3
2020	SLN	MLB	25	1.40	4.29	4.53	2.1	95.5	63.1	10.6	47.8

St. Louis Cardinals 2020

Dakota Hudson, continued

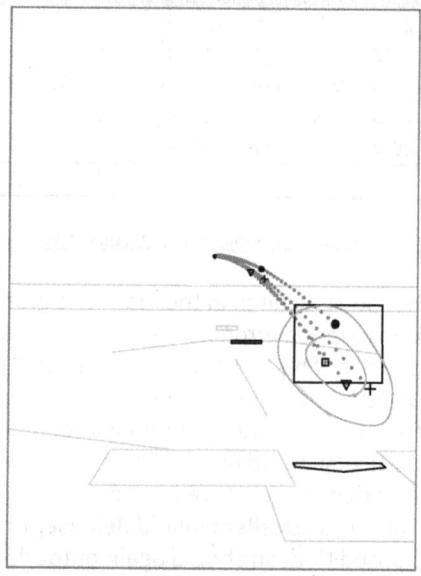

Type	Frequency	Velocity	H Movement	V Movement
● Fastball	13.8%	94.3 [105]	-4.3 [111]	-17.3 [97]
□ Sinker	47.9%	93.9 [107]	-11.2 [109]	-21.1 [98]
+ Cutter	25.6%	87.8 [94]	2.4 [103]	-30.7 [75]
▲ Changeup				
✕ Splitter				
▽ Slider	10.1%	82.3 [91]	8.4 [114]	-38.8 [83]
◇ Curveball				
✢ Slow Curveball				
✳ Knuckleball				
▼ Screwball				

Carlos Martínez   RHP

Born: 09/21/91   Age: 28   Bats: R   Throws: R
Height: 6'0"   Weight: 190   Origin: International Free Agent, 2009

YEAR	TEAM	LVL	AGE	W	L	SV	G	GS	IP	H	HR	BB/9	K/9	K	GB%	BABIP
2017	SLN	MLB	25	12	11	0	32	32	205	179	27	3.1	9.5	217	52%	.285
2018	SFD	AA	26	0	0	0	3	1	7	6	3	0.0	7.7	6	29%	.167
2018	SLN	MLB	26	8	6	5	33	18	118^2	100	5	4.6	8.9	117	51%	.290
2019	SLN	MLB	27	4	2	24	48	0	48^1	39	2	3.4	9.9	53	59%	.298
2020	SLN	MLB	28	3	3	31	53	0	56	51	6	3.8	10.1	63	54%	.307

Comparables: Danny Salazar, Jaime García, Yovani Gallardo

Last season was another round of everyone's favorite game "What Should We Make of Martínez?" This spin, he became a full-time reliever for the first time since his rookie year and anchored an excellent bullpen. He also added velocity to every pitch, scrapped his cutter, and emphasized his slider and changeup, his two best pitches. That all sounds awesome—and while it was, the context makes it bittersweet. The Cardinals see Martínez as a top-end starter, but fate keeps conspiring against him, with injuries keeping him from ascending to the elite status that looked nearly guaranteed earlier in his career. The 2019 season was proof that even a diminished Martínez is an excellent pitcher. But make no mistake—it was a disappointing season, and one that put yet more distance between him and his desired destination.

YEAR	TEAM	LVL	AGE	WHIP	ERA	DRA	WARP	MPH	FB%	WHF	CSP
2017	SLN	MLB	25	1.22	3.64	3.43	4.9	99.1	56.3	11.6	50.8
2018	SFD	AA	26	0.86	3.86	4.58	0.0				
2018	SLN	MLB	26	1.35	3.11	4.63	0.9	97.5	44.2	11.7	48.9
2019	SLN	MLB	27	1.18	3.17	3.29	1.1	98.6	51	14.3	47.4
2020	SLN	MLB	28	1.34	3.95	4.16	0.8	97.8	51.1	12.2	49

St. Louis Cardinals 2020

Carlos Martínez, continued

Pitch Shape vs LHH **Pitch Shape vs RHH**

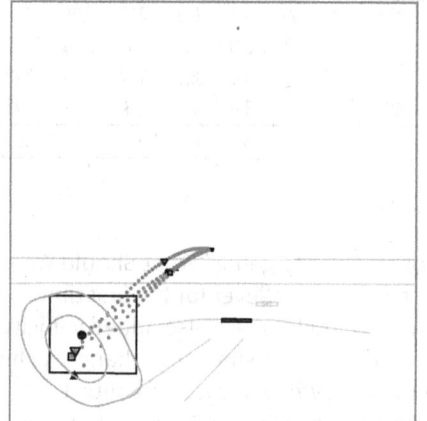
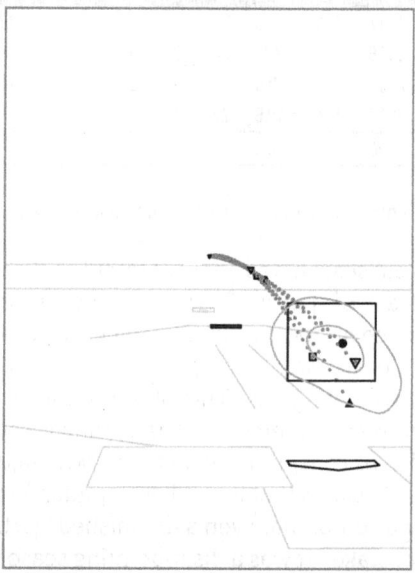

Type	Frequency	Velocity	H Movement	V Movement
● Fastball	30.3%	96.7 [112]	-7.8 [96]	-15.1 [102]
□ Sinker	20.7%	94.4 [109]	-14.4 [89]	-24.2 [86]
+ Cutter				
▲ Changeup	18.5%	88.2 [111]	-13.1 [91]	-32.9 [84]
× Splitter				
▽ Slider	28.4%	86.1 [107]	7.8 [112]	-30.6 [107]
◇ Curveball				
✤ Slow Curveball				
✳ Knuckleball				
▼ Screwball				

Miles Mikolas   RHP

Born: 08/23/88   Age: 31   Bats: R   Throws: R
Height: 6'5"   Weight: 220   Origin: Round 7, 2009 Draft (#204 overall)

YEAR	TEAM	LVL	AGE	W	L	SV	G	GS	IP	H	HR	BB/9	K/9	K	GB%	BABIP
2018	SLN	MLB	29	18	4	0	32	32	200^2	186	16	1.3	6.5	146	51%	.279
2019	SLN	MLB	30	9	14	0	32	32	184	193	27	1.6	7.0	144	49%	.302
2020	SLN	MLB	31	10	10	0	29	29	169	174	23	1.9	7.1	133	48%	.296

Comparables: Chase Whitley, Scott Feldman, Johnny Barbato

Mikolas was demoted from Lizard King to Lizard Prince last year, but his contract was boosted from princely to kingly, which means his season was a win on the whole. If you look past the royal nickname and blowout 2018, though, Mikolas makes a lot more sense. He's an above-average pitcher who gets there by keeping the ball on the ground and avoiding free passes. That kind of profile has a capped upside, but it also provides stability—potentially a high level. Mikolas isn't anyone's idea of an ace. He would be welcomed in every contender's rotation, however, and should be up to the challenge of validating his lucrative new deal over the coming seasons.

YEAR	TEAM	LVL	AGE	WHIP	ERA	DRA	WARP	MPH	FB%	WHF	CSP
2018	SLN	MLB	29	1.07	2.83	3.38	4.5	96.5	48.6	10.5	51.8
2019	SLN	MLB	30	1.22	4.16	4.14	3.3	96.0	51.5	10.7	48.8
2020	SLN	MLB	31	1.24	3.96	4.35	2.8	95.4	49.8	10.6	49.8

St. Louis Cardinals 2020

Miles Mikolas, continued

Pitch Shape vs LHH

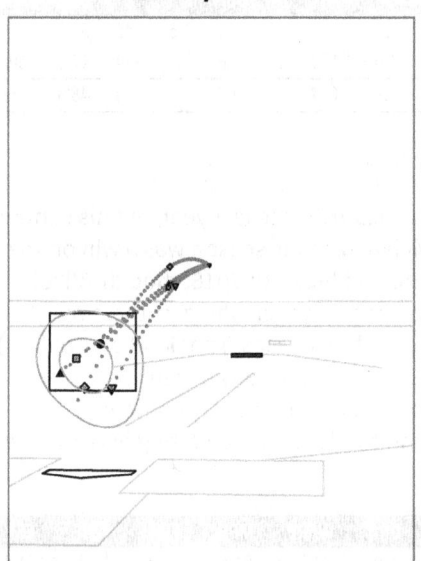

Pitch Shape vs RHH

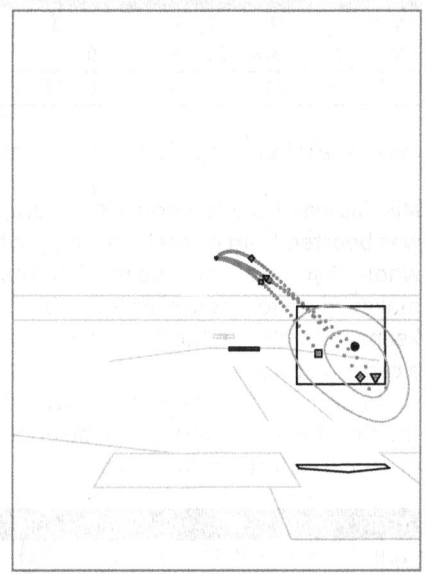

Type	Frequency	Velocity	H Movement	V Movement
● Fastball	27.4%	94 [105]	-4.9 [109]	-14.5 [104]
☐ Sinker	24.1%	93.8 [106]	-11.9 [105]	-17.4 [110]
+ Cutter				
▲ Changeup	3.6%	88.1 [110]	-12.3 [95]	-25.7 [105]
✕ Splitter				
▽ Slider	23.5%	87.3 [112]	3.6 [94]	-29.9 [109]
◇ Curveball	21.4%	78.6 [100]	8.2 [103]	-53.3 [88]
✦ Slow Curveball				
✱ Knuckleball				
▼ Screwball				

Andrew Miller LHP

Born: 05/21/85 Age: 35 Bats: L Throws: L
Height: 6'7" Weight: 205 Origin: Round 1, 2006 Draft (#6 overall)

YEAR	TEAM	LVL	AGE	W	L	SV	G	GS	IP	H	HR	BB/9	K/9	K	GB%	BABIP
2017	CLE	MLB	32	4	3	2	57	0	62^2	31	3	3.0	13.6	95	42%	.233
2018	CLE	MLB	33	2	4	2	37	0	34	31	3	4.2	11.9	45	50%	.329
2019	SLN	MLB	34	5	6	6	73	0	54^2	45	11	4.4	11.5	70	38%	.283
2020	SLN	MLB	35	3	2	7	53	0	56	42	7	3.2	11.8	73	42%	.274

Comparables: Arthur Rhodes, Brian Matusz, J.P. Howell

It's a good thing the term "Andrew Miller-type role" never stuck to describe high-leverage firemen, because it would be all kinds of confusing now that Miller himself is no longer fit for the role. It's not that he's bad; he still struck out nearly 30 percent of opposing batters, still befuddled lefties, and still posted a better-than-average DRA. It's just that he's not the same anymore; not the guy who was nigh unhittable for two years, whose slider starred in the nightmares of AL Central opponents. That's how the passage of time works, but it's jarring to see a diminished Miller, and more unnerving still to picture him three years down the road, surviving at the back of a bullpen on sheer guile.

YEAR	TEAM	LVL	AGE	WHIP	ERA	DRA	WARP	MPH	FB%	WHF	CSP
2017	CLE	MLB	32	0.83	1.44	2.30	2.0	97.3	41.9	17.1	45.7
2018	CLE	MLB	33	1.38	4.24	3.08	0.7	95.9	43.3	13.7	50.2
2019	SLN	MLB	34	1.32	4.45	3.73	1.0	95.6	38.6	13.7	48.7
2020	SLN	MLB	35	1.11	3.06	3.41	1.2	95.0	39.9	14.5	47.6

St. Louis Cardinals 2020

Andrew Miller, continued

Pitch Shape vs LHH

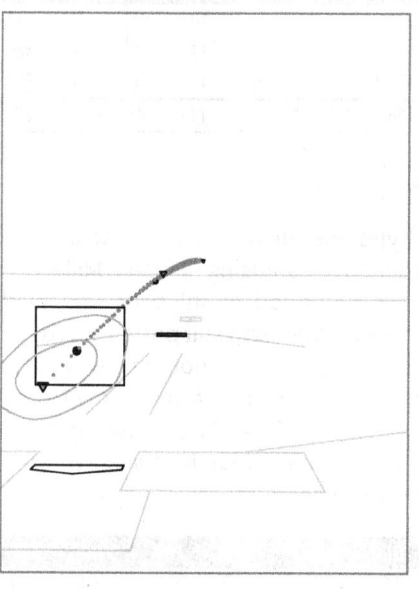

Pitch Shape vs RHH

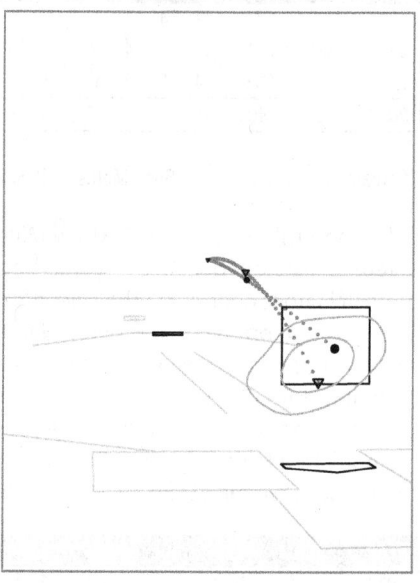

Type	Frequency	Velocity	H Movement	V Movement
● Fastball	38.1%	92.8 [101]	6.9 [100]	-15.8 [100]
☐ Sinker				
+ Cutter				
▲ Changeup				
✕ Splitter				
▽ Slider	61.4%	82.7 [93]	-9.6 [119]	-36 [91]
◇ Curveball				
⊕ Slow Curveball				
✱ Knuckleball				
▼ Screwball				

Adam Wainwright RHP

Born: 08/30/81   Age: 38   Bats: R   Throws: R
Height: 6'7"   Weight: 235   Origin: Round 1, 2000 Draft (#29 overall)

YEAR	TEAM	LVL	AGE	W	L	SV	G	GS	IP	H	HR	BB/9	K/9	K	GB%	BABIP
2017	SLN	MLB	35	12	5	0	24	23	123^1	140	14	3.3	7.0	96	50%	.326
2018	SFD	AA	36	1	0	0	3	3	10	5	0	0.0	8.1	9	42%	.192
2018	MEM	AAA	36	1	0	0	2	2	9	8	0	4.0	11.0	11	38%	.381
2018	SLN	MLB	36	2	4	0	8	8	40^1	41	5	4.0	8.9	40	51%	.310
2019	SLN	MLB	37	14	10	0	31	31	171^2	181	22	3.4	8.0	153	49%	.319
2020	SLN	MLB	38	9	9	0	26	26	143	147	20	2.9	7.7	122	48%	.303

Comparables: Jim Bunning, Gaylord Perry, Curt Schilling

If there's any justice in the world, Wainwright's 2019 will be remembered for his valiant effort in the playoffs, when he twice pitched into the eighth inning having allowed one or fewer runs. Unfortunately, the world isn't just: the Cardinals lost both of those games, and also lost the game where Wainwright pitched in relief on short rest. Even without the postseason heroics, however, 2019 would have been a satisfying bounceback for the Cardinals' former ace. He made 30 starts for only the second time in five years, adapting to his declining fastball velocity by throwing his curveball nearly 40 percent of the time, essentially a mirror image of his 2018 but over more innings. The end of the line isn't far away, but Wainwright's late-career renaissance is a welcome sight for the team and fans alike. He signed a one-year deal worth $5 million early in the offseason, and it shouldn't shock anyone if this is his farewell tour.

YEAR	TEAM	LVL	AGE	WHIP	ERA	DRA	WARP	MPH	FB%	WHF	CSP
2017	SLN	MLB	35	1.50	5.11	4.84	1.0	92.6	46.8	7.8	47.5
2018	SFD	AA	36	0.50	0.00	2.33	0.3				
2018	MEM	AAA	36	1.33	0.00	3.94	0.2				
2018	SLN	MLB	36	1.46	4.46	3.78	0.7	92.3	38	9.6	45.5
2019	SLN	MLB	37	1.43	4.19	4.58	2.2	91.9	38.5	8.2	48.5
2020	SLN	MLB	38	1.36	4.34	4.62	1.9	90.7	39.6	8	46

Adam Wainwright, continued

Pitch Shape vs LHH

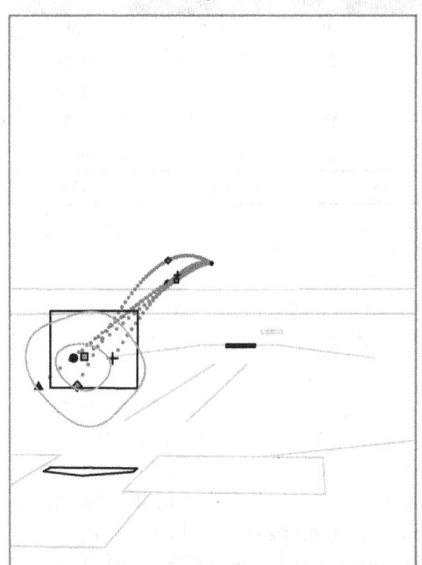

Pitch Shape vs RHH

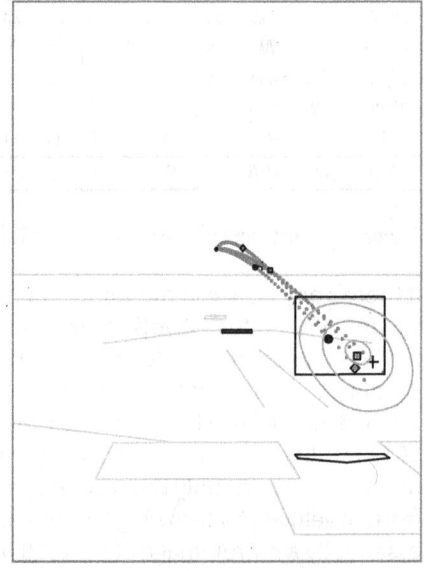

Type	Frequency	Velocity	H Movement	V Movement
● Fastball	13.7%	90 [93]	-2.5 [119]	-18 [95]
☐ Sinker	24.8%	90.3 [88]	-11.3 [108]	-21.5 [96]
+ Cutter	22.6%	85.1 [78]	5.2 [120]	-28.5 [84]
▲ Changeup				
✕ Splitter				
▽ Slider				
◇ Curveball	36.8%	75.2 [89]	16.7 [138]	-55.4 [83]
✦ Slow Curveball				
✱ Knuckleball				
▼ Screwball				

PLAYER COMMENTS WITHOUT GRAPHS

Luken Baker   1B
Born: 03/10/97   Age: 23   Bats: R   Throws: R
Height: 6'4"   Weight: 265   Origin: Round 2C, 2018 Draft (#75 overall)

YEAR	TEAM	LVL	AGE	PA	R	2B	3B	HR	RBI	BB	K	SB	CS	AVG/OBP/SLG
2018	CRD	RK	21	28	10	2	0	1	7	3	4	0	0	.500/.536/.708
2018	PEO	A	21	156	16	9	0	3	15	16	31	0	0	.288/.359/.417
2019	PMB	A+	22	496	47	32	1	10	53	52	112	1	1	.244/.327/.390
2020	SLN	MLB	23	251	25	13	0	8	29	17	71	1	0	.230/.286/.393

Comparables: Mark Trumbo, Nate Lowe, Matt Thaiss

When people make snide comments about baseball not requiring athleticism, they're thinking of players who look like Baker. He's listed at 6-foot-4 and 265 pounds, and plays just like it. He has light-tower power, a lot of swing-and-miss, and first-base-only defensive chops. And you know what? Watching someone of Baker's size play baseball is a *delight*. He doesn't quite look like Aaron Judge out there, but he still gives off the vibe an adult playing against children. Baker will have to keep hitting to make it to the majors. That means passing the Double-A test in 2020.

YEAR	TEAM	LVL	AGE	PA	DRC+	VORP	BABIP	BRR	FRAA	WARP
2018	CRD	RK	21	28	212	3.9	.550	-0.7	1B(5): 0.1	0.2
2018	PEO	A	21	156	148	2.7	.349	-1.4	1B(20): 0.3	0.8
2019	PMB	A+	22	496	118	4.7	.304	-6.1	1B(96): -3.6	0.3
2020	SLN	MLB	23	251	78	0.4	.296	-0.5	1B -1	-0.1

St. Louis Cardinals 2020

Dylan Carlson OF
Born: 10/23/98 Age: 21 Bats: B Throws: L
Height: 6'3" Weight: 205 Origin: Round 1, 2016 Draft (#33 overall)

YEAR	TEAM	LVL	AGE	PA	R	2B	3B	HR	RBI	BB	K	SB	CS	AVG/OBP/SLG
2017	PEO	A	18	451	63	18	1	7	42	52	116	6	6	.240/.342/.347
2018	PEO	A	19	57	5	3	0	2	9	10	10	2	0	.234/.368/.426
2018	PMB	A+	19	441	63	19	3	9	53	52	78	6	3	.247/.345/.386
2019	SFD	AA	20	483	81	24	6	21	59	52	98	18	7	.281/.364/.518
2019	MEM	AAA	20	79	14	4	2	5	9	6	18	2	1	.361/.418/.681
2020	SLN	MLB	21	140	16	6	1	5	18	12	38	0	0	.238/.312/.427

Comparables: Nomar Mazara, Victor Robles, Yorman Rodriguez

Carslon feels like he's been in the Cardinals system for a decade. He hasn't—he just turned 21. As a young draft pick, he's been afforded the opportunity to partake in four professional seasons. Progress isn't always linear, but it has been here since each season has surpassed its predecessor. Last year, Carlson overwhelmed the Texas League before putting up even better numbers in a Triple-A cameo. Combine his high level of production against older competition with his plus physical skills—easy switch-hitting power and enough athleticism that he's stuck in center field much longer than scouts expected—and it stands to reason that he'll do more than knock on the big-league door in 2020, and that he might spend a decade on the Cards' 26-man roster.

YEAR	TEAM	LVL	AGE	PA	DRC+	VORP	BABIP	BRR	FRAA	WARP
2017	PEO	A	18	451	98	14.6	.323	2.6	RF(79): 0.8, CF(24): 0.1	1.4
2018	PEO	A	19	57	137	1.4	.257	-0.7	RF(10): 2.3, CF(4): -0.3	0.5
2018	PMB	A+	19	441	115	18.2	.286	1.7	RF(50): 4.7, LF(37): -0.1	2.1
2019	SFD	AA	20	483	151	40.3	.315	3.1	CF(86): -10.2, RF(9): -0.3	2.7
2019	MEM	AAA	20	79	142	10.9	.429	0.1	CF(8): -0.5, LF(7): 0.0	0.6
2020	SLN	MLB	21	140	96	2.5	.297	0.0	LF 0, RF -1	0.2

Trejyn Fletcher OF

Born: 04/30/01   Age: 19   Bats: R   Throws: R
Height: 6'2"   Weight: 200   Origin: Round 2, 2019 Draft (#58 overall)

YEAR	TEAM	LVL	AGE	PA	R	2B	3B	HR	RBI	BB	K	SB	CS	AVG/OBP/SLG
2019	CRD	RK	18	42	6	3	0	2	8	4	17	0	0	.297/.357/.541
2019	JCY	RK+	18	133	9	4	1	2	18	7	59	7	1	.228/.271/.325
2020	SLN	MLB	19	251	21	11	1	4	22	19	128	2	1	.201/.266/.310

Comparables: Colby Rasmus, Addison Russell, Bo Bichette

Maine isn't a baseball hotbed, particularly at the prep level—only three Maine high schoolers have ever been taken in the first round in draft history. When Fletcher transferred to Portland and reclassified to the 2019 draft, scouts had to scramble to see him play. That led to him slipping to the second round, which could prove to be a steal on the Cardinals' part. He's a 6-foot-2 livewire on the field, with speed and strength to burn. His performance? Hey, we needn't discuss that more at this point than to acknowledge the learning curve that comes with transitioning from facing Maine pitching to professionals. It wasn't pretty, in other words, but Fletcher has the tools to make up for it over the coming years.

YEAR	TEAM	LVL	AGE	PA	DRC+	VORP	BABIP	BRR	FRAA	WARP
2019	CRD	RK	18	42	92	2.1	.474	0.0	CF(7): 2.2	0.3
2019	JCY	RK+	18	133	63	-3.3	.406	-0.2		-0.1
2020	SLN	MLB	19	251	55	-6.8	.425	0.0	CF 1	-0.6

St. Louis Cardinals 2020

Nolan Gorman 3B

Born: 05/10/00   Age: 20   Bats: L   Throws: R
Height: 6'1"   Weight: 210   Origin: Round 1, 2018 Draft (#19 overall)

YEAR	TEAM	LVL	AGE	PA	R	2B	3B	HR	RBI	BB	K	SB	CS	AVG/OBP/SLG
2018	JCY	RK	18	167	41	10	1	11	28	24	37	1	3	.350/.443/.664
2018	PEO	A	18	107	8	3	0	6	16	10	39	0	2	.202/.280/.426
2019	PEO	A	19	282	41	14	3	10	41	32	79	2	0	.241/.344/.448
2019	PMB	A+	19	230	24	16	3	5	21	13	73	0	1	.256/.304/.428
2020	SLN	MLB	20	251	26	12	1	8	29	24	86	1	0	.222/.302/.393

Comparables: Miguel Sanó, Austin Riley, Gary Sánchez

Gorman has established a pattern. In 2018, he was simply too good for rookie ball, so the team challenged him with a promotion to Low-A, where he saw his strikeouts spike but hit for enough power to make the whole package work. He started in Low-A last year and cut his strikeouts while walking more, showing the team enough that they tasked him with the Florida State League…where he, as the youngest regular, struggled with strikeouts but hit for enough power to be an above-average hitter. (Note to the universe: Get more creative writers, won't you?) If the trend holds, Gorman will begin the year in Double-A, dominate, then try to slug enough to atone for his strikeout sins. The upside here is something like a lesser Joey Gallo if Joey Gallo liked playing third base. We think the old-timers called it "Russell Branyan."

YEAR	TEAM	LVL	AGE	PA	DRC+	VORP	BABIP	BRR	FRAA	WARP
2018	JCY	RK	18	167	191	25.2	.411	-0.7	3B(33): 7.6	2.7
2018	PEO	A	18	107	76	2.3	.255	-0.5	3B(25): 3.9	0.5
2019	PEO	A	19	282	129	16.9	.312	0.4	3B(51): 8.4	2.6
2019	PMB	A+	19	230	107	6.7	.365	-2.1	3B(48): -5.9	0.0
2020	SLN	MLB	20	251	84	2.7	.320	-0.4	3B 1	0.4

Ivan Herrera   C

Born: 06/01/00   Age: 20   Bats: R   Throws: R
Height: 6'0"   Weight: 180   Origin: International Free Agent, 2016

YEAR	TEAM	LVL	AGE	PA	R	2B	3B	HR	RBI	BB	K	SB	CS	AVG/OBP/SLG
2017	DCA	RK	17	201	21	15	0	1	27	18	36	2	2	.335/.425/.441
2018	CRD	RK	18	130	23	6	4	1	25	11	20	1	1	.348/.423/.500
2019	PEO	A	19	291	41	10	0	8	42	35	56	1	1	.286/.381/.423
2019	PMB	A+	19	65	7	0	0	1	5	5	16	0	0	.276/.338/.328
2020	SLN	MLB	20	251	26	11	1	6	27	19	66	1	0	.258/.325/.392

Comparables: Victor Robles, J.P. Crawford, César Puello

The Arizona Fall League is purportedly a showcase for some of the best prospects in baseball, which means it provides a higher level of competition than younger players are accustomed to facing. So, when you go there and absolutely rake as a 19-year-old—a 19-year-old catcher, no less—it's bound to create waves. Herrera did just that, completing a season in which he also held his head above water in the Florida State League—notoriously a pitcher's paradise. Teenage catchers are always a high-variance quantity, and Herrera is a ways away from being a big-league ready defensive backstop. But his bat is promising and if he can do enough to stick behind the dish then he has a bright future ahead.

YEAR	TEAM	LVL	AGE	PA	DRC+	VORP	BABIP	BRR	FRAA	WARP
2017	DCA	RK	17	201	144	19.5	.415	-0.5	C(49): 0.7	1.9
2018	CRD	RK	18	130	154	11.6	.409	-1.9	C(20): 0.6	1.0
2019	PEO	A	19	291	138	21.7	.337	-0.1	C(64): -1.0	2.4
2019	PMB	A+	19	65	117	2.5	.357	-1.1	C(17): -0.1	0.3
2020	SLN	MLB	20	251	92	5.3	.339	-0.3	C -1	0.5

Andrew Knizner C

Born: 02/03/95 Age: 25 Bats: R Throws: R
Height: 6'1" Weight: 200 Origin: Round 7, 2016 Draft (#226 overall)

YEAR	TEAM	LVL	AGE	PA	R	2B	3B	HR	RBI	BB	K	SB	CS	AVG/OBP/SLG
2017	PEO	A	22	191	18	10	1	8	29	9	22	1	1	.279/.325/.480
2017	SFD	AA	22	202	27	13	0	4	22	14	27	0	1	.324/.371/.462
2018	SFD	AA	23	313	39	13	0	7	41	23	40	0	1	.313/.365/.434
2018	MEM	AAA	23	61	3	5	0	0	4	4	8	0	0	.315/.383/.407
2019	MEM	AAA	24	280	41	10	0	12	34	24	37	2	0	.276/.357/.463
2019	SLN	MLB	24	58	7	2	0	2	7	4	14	2	0	.226/.293/.377
2020	SLN	MLB	25	182	19	7	0	6	21	12	34	0	0	.242/.306/.388

Comparables: AJ Hinch, Randy Knorr, Hal King

With Carson Kelly dealt elsewhere, Knizner became the Cardinals' top catching prospect and the next young backstop to have his arrival delayed by Yadier Molina's remarkable durability. Knizer's offensive profile is unusual for a catcher, as it's all bat control and middling power. That combination has served him well in the minor leagues so far, but it's fair to be skeptical about anyone, let alone a slow-footed catcher, being able to sustain an offensive game based around singles. Without a huge offensive ceiling, defense—specifically framing—may decide whether Knizner is a regular or backup. While he's been up-and-down on that front since converting from third base, he'll get some more time in Triple-A to learn the trade before Molina's contract expires.

YEAR	TEAM	P. COUNT	FRM RUNS	BLK RUNS	THRW RUNS	TOT RUNS
2017	SFD	6878	-3.0	0.0	0.2	-3.9
2018	MEM	2067	1.9	0.2	-0.1	1.9
2018	SFD	10157	-3.7	-1.9	-0.1	-6.0
2019	MEM	9240	-18.8	-0.1	1.7	-17.1
2019	SLN	2077	-4.0	-0.4	0.1	-4.0
2020	SLN	6472	-9.6	-0.6	0.8	-9.4

YEAR	TEAM	LVL	AGE	PA	DRC+	VORP	BABIP	BRR	FRAA	WARP
2017	PEO	A	22	191	124	13.5	.282	0.5	C(26): -0.3, 1B(3): -0.1	1.1
2017	SFD	AA	22	202	145	18.7	.355	0.5	C(49): -3.5	1.5
2018	SFD	AA	23	313	133	21.9	.339	-1.4	C(74): -7.3	1.6
2018	MEM	AAA	23	61	115	3.8	.370	-0.1	C(16): 1.8	0.6
2019	MEM	AAA	24	280	112	21.8	.281	-0.8	C(61): -17.2	0.2
2019	SLN	MLB	24	58	82	1.7	.270	0.5	C(16): -4.4, 1B(1): 0.0	-0.2
2020	SLN	MLB	25	182	88	5.2	.274	-0.4	C -10	-0.5

Elehuris Montero 3B

Born: 08/17/98 Age: 21 Bats: R Throws: R
Height: 6'3" Weight: 215 Origin: International Free Agent, 2014

YEAR	TEAM	LVL	AGE	PA	R	2B	3B	HR	RBI	BB	K	SB	CS	AVG/OBP/SLG
2017	CRD	RK	18	208	30	16	1	5	36	22	33	0	2	.277/.370/.468
2018	PEO	A	19	425	68	28	3	15	69	33	81	2	0	.322/.381/.529
2018	PMB	A+	19	106	13	9	0	1	13	5	22	1	0	.286/.330/.408
2019	SFD	AA	20	238	23	8	0	7	18	14	74	0	1	.188/.235/.317
2020	SLN	MLB	21	251	23	13	0	7	27	14	81	0	0	.221/.272/.370

Comparables: Jorge Polanco, Miguel Andújar, Jonathan Schoop

If you're curious about why Double-A is considered the hardest step in the minor-league ladder, look no further than Montero. He was one of the hottest hitting prospects in baseball last year. He even held his own when promoted to the offense-suppressing Palm Beach affiliate. Montero started 2019 in Double-A, and baseball got very hard for him in no time at all. Pitchers knocked the bat out of his hands; he struck out almost a third of the time; he rarely walked; and he posted poor average and power numbers. His second year at the level will give him a chance to improve, but it's always perilous to project offensive performance based on A-ball stats. Montero's 2019 is an excellent example of why.

YEAR	TEAM	LVL	AGE	PA	DRC+	VORP	BABIP	BRR	FRAA	WARP
2017	CRD	RK	18	208	141	10.8	.305	-0.5	3B(41): 2.8	1.5
2018	PEO	A	19	425	169	39.7	.372	0.3	3B(77): 2.7	4.6
2018	PMB	A+	19	106	118	5.7	.355	0.6	3B(20): 0.8	0.6
2019	SFD	AA	20	238	34	-5.4	.245	-0.4	3B(51): -6.2	-1.4
2020	SLN	MLB	21	251	70	-2.0	.306	-0.4	3B -3	-0.5

St. Louis Cardinals 2020

Malcom Nunez 3B
Born: 03/09/01 Age: 19 Bats: R Throws: R
Height: 5'11" Weight: 205 Origin: International Free Agent, 2017

YEAR	TEAM	LVL	AGE	PA	R	2B	3B	HR	RBI	BB	K	SB	CS	AVG/OBP/SLG
2018	DCA	RK	17	199	44	16	2	13	59	26	29	3	0	.415/.497/.774
2019	JCY	RK+	18	146	14	11	0	2	13	13	32	3	2	.254/.336/.385
2019	PEO	A	18	77	5	1	0	0	5	5	15	0	0	.183/.247/.197
2020	SLN	MLB	19	251	22	13	1	3	22	23	73	0	0	.222/.299/.328

Comparables: Jefry Marte, Anthony Santander, Alex Liddi

Nunez was so good in the DSL that the Cardinals gave him an aggressive promotion to Low-A Peoria, where he was more than three years younger than the average player. He struggled there and the Cardinals moved him down, but it would be wise to cut him some slack. After all, within the past year he: moved to the U.S.; played a more grueling schedule; and faced far older opposition for the first time. Even with those caveats noted, Nunez's profile raises red flags for a player scouts see as an early bloomer. There's a chance he ends up as a first-base-only prospect given his build, in turn putting significant pressure on his bat. That's not disqualifying—his bat has a chance to be special, with plus feel for hit and power—but between his defensive limitations and his distance from the big leagues, it's premature to consider him the Cardinals' next big thing.

YEAR	TEAM	LVL	AGE	PA	DRC+	VORP	BABIP	BRR	FRAA	WARP
2018	DCA	RK	17	199	225	37.1	.437	0.5	3B(30): -1.0, 1B(5): 1.2	3.2
2019	JCY	RK+	18	146	108	4.1	.323	-0.4		0.6
2019	PEO	A	18	77	56	-7.2	.232	-1.8	3B(8): 0.0	-0.4
2020	SLN	MLB	19	251	71	-1.6	.312	-0.3	3B -1, 1B 0	-0.3

Rangel Ravelo 1B

Born: 04/24/92   Age: 28   Bats: R   Throws: R
Height: 6'1"   Weight: 225   Origin: Round 6, 2010 Draft (#188 overall)

YEAR	TEAM	LVL	AGE	PA	R	2B	3B	HR	RBI	BB	K	SB	CS	AVG/OBP/SLG
2017	MEM	AAA	25	345	49	25	1	8	41	31	56	1	2	.314/.383/.480
2018	MEM	AAA	26	399	57	19	2	13	67	42	49	0	1	.308/.392/.487
2019	MEM	AAA	27	381	50	20	1	12	56	37	61	0	1	.299/.383/.473
2019	SLN	MLB	27	43	4	2	0	2	7	3	12	0	0	.205/.256/.410
2020	SLN	MLB	28	49	5	2	0	1	6	4	10	0	0	.241/.316/.391

Comparables: Ji-Man Choi, Joey Terdoslavich, José Osuna

Ravelo fits an interesting, oft-disregarded archetype: the right-right first baseman who puts up excellent offensive numbers despite middling power. The comparisons to Luke Voit are too easy to ignore. Like Voit, he's received few opportunities at the major-league level despite repeatedly performing in the minors. Unlike Voit, his batted-ball profile limits his ceiling—he hits too many grounders and, even with the altered ball in Triple-A this year, he could manage only 12 home runs. His low strikeout totals offset his lack of power, but the overall package isn't what you would hope for a player with his defensive limitations. As such, Ravelo's best chance is to be spun elsewhere, perhaps to a rebuilding team seeking a Voit of their own.

YEAR	TEAM	LVL	AGE	PA	DRC+	VORP	BABIP	BRR	FRAA	WARP
2017	MEM	AAA	25	345	131	20.9	.359	-2.9	1B(52): 0.0, RF(12): 0.2	1.6
2018	MEM	AAA	26	399	135	29.0	.328	0.6	1B(54): 3.6, LF(36): -1.7	2.7
2019	MEM	AAA	27	381	118	17.8	.336	-0.3	1B(43): 1.4, LF(36): 2.9	1.9
2019	SLN	MLB	27	43	76	-0.3	.231	-0.1	1B(9): -0.5	-0.1
2020	SLN	MLB	28	49	91	0.6	.285	-0.1	1B 0	0.1

Jhon Torres OF

Born: 03/29/00 Age: 20 Bats: R Throws: R
Height: 6'4" Weight: 199 Origin: International Free Agent, 2016

YEAR	TEAM	LVL	AGE	PA	R	2B	3B	HR	RBI	BB	K	SB	CS	AVG/OBP/SLG
2017	DIN	RK	17	226	25	7	3	5	35	28	41	4	4	.255/.363/.408
2018	CLT	RK	18	111	16	3	0	4	16	11	24	3	0	.273/.351/.424
2018	CRD	RK	18	75	11	6	0	4	14	8	13	1	1	.397/.493/.683
2019	JCY	RK+	19	133	24	9	0	6	17	19	36	0	2	.286/.391/.527
2019	PEO	A	19	75	4	3	0	0	8	7	29	0	1	.167/.240/.212
2020	SLN	MLB	20	251	22	12	1	5	23	23	89	0	0	.211/.291/.329

Comparables: José Martínez, Abraham Almonte, Dilson Herrera

Your eyes aren't deceiving you: that H in Torres' first name appears aggressively early. Also aggressively early: his offensive production. He overpowered Gulf Coast and Appy League pitching in 2018 and 2019, with his feel to hit, his patience, and his raw power—a trio that made him look like a potential middle-of-the-order bat. There is one red flag worth disclosing: the Cardinals briefly sent him to the Midwest League to start the season, and he looked like—well, a 19-year-old in a tough league. Provided Torres does better in his second tour in the Midwest League, he could be in the big-league picture sooner than expected. Players with his combination of production and projection don't tend to hang around in the minors for long.

YEAR	TEAM	LVL	AGE	PA	DRC+	VORP	BABIP	BRR	FRAA	WARP
2017	DIN	RK	17	226	112	13.0	.290	-0.3	RF(29): -0.8, CF(22): -4.6	0.2
2018	CLT	RK	18	111	123	2.6	.324	-0.3	RF(24): 5.6, CF(1): -0.1	1.0
2018	CRD	RK	18	75	206	12.5	.457	0.2	RF(15): 5.2	1.3
2019	JCY	RK+	19	133	151	11.8	.366	0.8		1.1
2019	PEO	A	19	75	49	-4.5	.282	-0.6	RF(20): 3.8	0.1
2020	SLN	MLB	20	251	67	-2.9	.326	-0.4	RF 4, CF 0	0.0

Justin Williams OF

Born: 08/20/95   Age: 24   Bats: L   Throws: R
Height: 6'2"   Weight: 215   Origin: Round 2, 2013 Draft (#52 overall)

YEAR	TEAM	LVL	AGE	PA	R	2B	3B	HR	RBI	BB	K	SB	CS	AVG/OBP/SLG
2017	MNT	AA	21	409	53	21	3	14	72	37	69	6	2	.301/.364/.489
2018	DUR	AAA	22	386	41	18	0	8	46	25	81	4	3	.258/.313/.376
2018	MEM	AAA	22	76	8	3	0	3	11	5	17	0	1	.217/.276/.391
2018	TBA	MLB	22	1	0	0	0	0	0	0	0	0	0	.000/.000/.000
2019	SFD	AA	23	61	7	1	0	1	3	4	17	1	0	.193/.246/.263
2019	MEM	AAA	23	119	20	5	0	7	26	16	30	0	0	.353/.437/.608
2020	SLN	MLB	24	35	4	1	0	1	4	2	10	0	0	.235/.289/.379

Comparables: Xavier Avery, Gabriel Guerrero, Yorman Rodriguez

Thus far in his Cardinals career, Williams has a case of the second-bests. He was the second-best player the Birds received in return for Tommy Pham (after Génesis Cabrera), the second-best minor leaguer to hurt his hand punching something in frustration (after Alex Reyes), and is now the second-best lefty outfielder in Triple-A with Dylan Carlson also in tow. He doesn't do any one thing tremendously well, but he does a lot of things okay, which might earn him a swing role on the 2020 team—except, uh, Randy Arozarena does everything a little better, which makes Williams second-best there too. At least he's consistent?

YEAR	TEAM	LVL	AGE	PA	DRC+	VORP	BABIP	BRR	FRAA	WARP
2017	MNT	AA	21	409	147	18.6	.334	-2.0	RF(80): -4.8, LF(7): 1.2	2.1
2018	DUR	AAA	22	386	97	-4.9	.315	-2.7	RF(80): 13.7, LF(2): 1.0	1.8
2018	MEM	AAA	22	76	86	-0.6	.240	-1.1	LF(10): 4.2, RF(7): 0.9	0.5
2018	TBA	MLB	22	1	83	-0.5	.000	0.0	RF(1): 0.0	0.0
2019	SFD	AA	23	61	56	-2.3	.256	-0.1	LF(12): -0.7, RF(2): -0.1	-0.2
2019	MEM	AAA	23	119	146	14.2	.439	-0.5	RF(24): 3.9	1.2
2020	SLN	MLB	24	35	76	-0.4	.301	-0.1	RF 0	0.0

Seth Elledge RHP

Born: 05/20/96 Age: 24 Bats: R Throws: R
Height: 6'3" Weight: 240 Origin: Round 4, 2017 Draft (#123 overall)

YEAR	TEAM	LVL	AGE	W	L	SV	G	GS	IP	H	HR	BB/9	K/9	K	GB%	BABIP
2017	CLN	A	21	3	0	5	15	0	21	14	1	2.6	15.0	35	40%	.310
2018	MOD	A+	22	5	1	9	31	0	38^1	18	1	3.5	12.7	54	53%	.221
2018	SFD	AA	22	3	1	4	13	0	16^2	13	3	3.2	10.8	20	44%	.250
2019	SFD	AA	23	3	3	3	26	0	33^1	34	3	3.5	11.6	43	44%	.383
2019	MEM	AAA	23	3	1	0	21	3	34^1	28	3	5.0	8.4	32	41%	.287
2020	SLN	MLB	24	2	2	0	33	0	35	35	5	3.6	9.2	36	41%	.307

Comparables: Akeel Morris, Heath Hembree, Eduardo Paredes

When Elledge joined the Cardinals in a 2018 trade, they showed what they thought of him by promoting him to Double-A. They continued to show their belief in him last year, pushing him to Triple-A midway through the season and then sending him to Fall League. Elledge didn't disappoint, striking out more than a batter an inning with a strikeout-to-walk ratio of 6.00 in the showcase league. His pitch mix, featuring a mid-90s fastball and cookie-cutter slider, doesn't jump off the page, but he has a deceptive, long-striding delivery that keeps batters off-balance and causes both pitches to play up. Plug him into the big league bullpen, and he'd be a younger, near-clone of Sam Tuivailala, the guy he was traded for.

YEAR	TEAM	LVL	AGE	WHIP	ERA	DRA	WARP	MPH	FB%	WHF	CSP
2017	CLN	A	21	0.95	3.00	2.21	0.7				
2018	MOD	A+	22	0.86	1.17	1.52	1.5				
2018	SFD	AA	22	1.14	4.32	3.61	0.3				
2019	SFD	AA	23	1.41	3.78	5.22	-0.3				
2019	MEM	AAA	23	1.37	4.72	4.77	0.5				
2020	SLN	MLB	24	1.39	4.51	4.65	0.3				

Connor Jones RHP

Born: 10/10/94 Age: 25 Bats: R Throws: R
Height: 6'3" Weight: 220 Origin: Round 2, 2016 Draft (#70 overall)

YEAR	TEAM	LVL	AGE	W	L	SV	G	GS	IP	H	HR	BB/9	K/9	K	GB%	BABIP
2017	PMB	A+	22	8	5	1	24	21	113^1	120	3	3.9	6.0	76	69%	.321
2017	SFD	AA	22	1	0	0	1	1	6^2	6	1	4.1	2.7	2	71%	.250
2018	SFD	AA	23	5	5	0	22	17	94^2	96	4	4.8	6.3	66	64%	.309
2018	MEM	AAA	23	1	0	0	4	4	15^1	20	1	8.2	9.4	16	62%	.388
2019	SFD	AA	24	1	1	9	42	0	48^1	54	5	6.5	9.1	49	63%	.353
2020	SLN	MLB	25	2	2	0	33	0	35	33	5	4.0	6.7	26	56%	.274

Comparables: Pedro Payano, Jared Hughes, Chris Ellis

Jones made the switch from starting to relieving last season, an inevitable move given his spotty command. He was a lock for a few fastballs to the backstop and a few walks per game, as well as some nasty sinkers that batters couldn't square up. His first year of relief didn't go particularly well—he put on 15 percent of the batters he faced in Double-A—but he's a legitimate candidate to crack the big-league bullpen soon. His bowling-ball sinker continues to overpower batters, running into the upper-90s in short spurts and fueling a 63 percent groundball rate. Finding the strike zone with any regularity is the only thing standing between him and being a quality reliever.

YEAR	TEAM	LVL	AGE	WHIP	ERA	DRA	WARP	MPH	FB%	WHF	CSP
2017	PMB	A+	22	1.49	3.97	5.58	-0.5				
2017	SFD	AA	22	1.35	2.70	5.32	0.0				
2018	SFD	AA	23	1.55	3.80	5.93	-0.7				
2018	MEM	AAA	23	2.22	6.46	7.78	-0.4				
2019	SFD	AA	24	1.84	4.66	6.78	-1.3				
2020	SLN	MLB	25	1.39	4.40	4.55	0.3				

Kwang-Hyun Kim   LHP
Born: 07/02/88   Age: 31   Bats: L   Throws: L
Height: 6'2"   Weight: 185   Origin: International Free Agent, 2019

Depth and flexibility are two of the biggest buzzwords in baseball over the last few years, and the Cardinals acquired both when they signed Kim to a two-year, $8 million contract. The left-hander has the ability to start or relieve for a Cardinals team that could use some of both. He'll sit in the low-90s with an average slider, but Kim's best attribute is his ability to pound the zone. That alone might allow him to stick in the rotation, where he'll need to deploy his fringy changeup and get-me-over curve more frequently. The lack of a solid third pitch might have doomed him to the bullpen not so long ago, but Kim could find success as a two-time-through-the-order type in a starting role, now.

Evan Kruczynski LHP

Born: 03/31/95　Age: 25　Bats: L　Throws: L
Height: 6'5"　Weight: 215　Origin: Round 9, 2017 Draft (#274 overall)

YEAR	TEAM	LVL	AGE	W	L	SV	G	GS	IP	H	HR	BB/9	K/9	K	GB%	BABIP
2017	PEO	A	22	4	3	0	14	13	68^2	70	7	2.0	7.2	55	49%	.307
2018	PMB	A+	23	5	3	0	15	15	76	74	6	2.5	8.8	74	49%	.309
2018	SFD	AA	23	2	3	0	6	6	39^2	27	1	2.3	7.5	33	36%	.255
2019	SFD	AA	24	3	8	0	21	20	117^1	123	18	3.8	9.1	118	41%	.322
2019	MEM	AAA	24	1	2	0	7	6	30^1	44	3	5.0	8.3	28	33%	.414
2020	SLN	MLB	25	2	2	0	33	0	35	36	6	3.7	7.5	29	38%	.289

Comparables: Brandon Workman, Jacob Waguespack, Thomas Pannone

With Gregg Popovich now coaching the U.S. Olympic basketball team, Kruczynski has some extra free time. Duke recruiting practically runs itself, and there are more things in the world than sitting on the sidelines and looking exactly the same as you did 20 years earlier. So, what did he do? Why he took to baseball. On the right day, he can be found tossing a low-90s fastball and array of passable secondary pitches that should grant him life as a low-end major leaguer. Not bad for a 73-year-old.

YEAR	TEAM	LVL	AGE	WHIP	ERA	DRA	WARP	MPH	FB%	WHF	CSP
2017	PEO	A	22	1.24	3.41	4.88	0.3				
2018	PMB	A+	23	1.25	4.03	4.40	0.8				
2018	SFD	AA	23	0.93	2.50	2.80	1.2				
2019	SFD	AA	24	1.47	5.60	5.18	-0.4				
2019	MEM	AAA	24	2.01	8.01	7.56	-0.3				
2020	SLN	MLB	25	1.42	4.79	4.91	0.2				

Matthew Liberatore LHP

Born: 11/06/99 Age: 20 Bats: L Throws: L
Height: 6'5" Weight: 200 Origin: Round 1, 2018 Draft (#16 overall)

YEAR	TEAM	LVL	AGE	W	L	SV	G	GS	IP	H	HR	BB/9	K/9	K	GB%	BABIP
2018	RAY	RK	18	1	2	0	8	8	27^2	16	0	3.6	10.4	32	45%	.258
2019	BGR	A	19	6	2	0	16	15	78^1	70	2	3.6	8.7	76	58%	.311
2020	TBA	MLB	20	2	2	0	33	0	35	34	5	4.0	7.2	28	52%	.281

Comparables: Brad Hand, Jake Thompson, Eduardo Rodriguez

Arguably the top prep lefty in the 2018 draft, Liberatore made his full-season debut in 2019; a somewhat aggressive assignment by the conservative leaning Rays. He held up more than adequately as a 19-year-old in the Midwest League where most players are on average three years older than he was. He has a tall frame with the ability to fill out more as he matures. The southpaw tosses a four-pitch medley, led by a low-90s fastball that he can run higher when needed, a curveball that projects to be an out pitch, a changeup with similar projection to fend off the platoon split and a slider that he added along the way. He wraps it up with plus control that is solid enough to morph into plus command as he gains experience. He will likely spend most, if not all, of 2020 at the organization's spring training base in Port Charlotte, cutting his teeth in the muggy air of the Florida State League.

YEAR	TEAM	LVL	AGE	WHIP	ERA	DRA	WARP	MPH	FB%	WHF	CSP
2018	RAY	RK	18	0.98	0.98	2.03	1.2				
2019	BGR	A	19	1.29	3.10	4.78	0.4				
2020	TBA	MLB	20	1.40	4.50	4.64	0.2				

Alex Reyes   RHP

Born: 08/29/94   Age: 25   Bats: R   Throws: R
Height: 6'3"   Weight: 175   Origin: International Free Agent, 2012

YEAR	TEAM	LVL	AGE	W	L	SV	G	GS	IP	H	HR	BB/9	K/9	K	GB%	BABIP
2018	SFD	AA	23	1	0	0	1	1	7^2	1	0	3.5	15.3	13	30%	.100
2018	MEM	AAA	23	1	0	0	1	1	7	1	0	1.3	16.7	13	33%	.111
2018	SLN	MLB	23	0	0	0	1	1	4	3	0	4.5	4.5	2	40%	.300
2019	PMB	A+	24	0	1	0	2	2	9^1	9	0	2.9	10.6	11	54%	.346
2019	MEM	AAA	24	1	3	0	10	7	28	27	5	7.7	12.2	38	41%	.344
2019	SLN	MLB	24	0	1	0	4	0	3	2	1	18.0	3.0	1	30%	.111
2020	SLN	MLB	25	3	4	0	38	6	66	69	10	6.1	7.1	52	35%	.296

Comparables: Rafael Montero, Aaron Sanchez, Neftalí Feliz

The wait for Reyes is threatening to eclipse that for Godot. He's been on the cusp of making it big since 2016, when he debuted in August and was electric in a hybrid role. From then on, it's been pratfalls and banana peels for Reyes; a UCL tear erased his 2017 season, and a shoulder injury he suffered while rehabbing spoke for 2018. Last season brought another mixture of injuries and ineffectiveness, including a two-for-one: Reyes broke his hand while punching a wall in frustration. The only silver lining for Reyes is that he was on the major-league roster for two of the last three seasons, accumulating service time and a major-league minimum salary. It's a small mercy, to be sure, but one that feels deserved after his poor run of luck.

YEAR	TEAM	LVL	AGE	WHIP	ERA	DRA	WARP	MPH	FB%	WHF	CSP
2018	SFD	AA	23	0.52	0.00	1.48	0.3				
2018	MEM	AAA	23	0.29	0.00	1.34	0.3				
2018	SLN	MLB	23	1.25	0.00	8.15	-0.1	97.4	57.5	4.1	43
2019	PMB	A+	24	1.29	1.93	3.65	0.2				
2019	MEM	AAA	24	1.82	7.39	5.18	0.4				
2019	SLN	MLB	24	2.67	15.00	6.67	0.0	99.1	59.4	5.8	42.2
2020	SLN	MLB	25	1.72	5.92	5.76	-0.1	97.9	60	5.1	43.6

Griffin Roberts RHP

Born: 06/13/96 Age: 24 Bats: R Throws: R
Height: 6'3" Weight: 205 Origin: Round 1, 2018 Draft (#43 overall)

YEAR	TEAM	LVL	AGE	W	L	SV	G	GS	IP	H	HR	BB/9	K/9	K	GB%	BABIP
2018	CRD	RK	22	0	1	1	7	2	8^2	6	0	4.2	11.4	11	55%	.300
2019	PMB	A+	23	1	7	0	15	13	65^2	79	3	4.8	4.9	36	49%	.338
2020	SLN	MLB	24	2	2	0	33	0	35	35	5	4.1	4.6	18	45%	.264

Comparables: John Cornely, Jose A. Valdez, Mike Hauschild

It's high time the Cardinals start treating Roberts as an impact reliever rather than a starter. A summer spent weeding out some of the inconsistencies in his game explains his poor statline in High-A, but it can't explain the decreased velocity he showed, both there and in the Fall League. The fastball was down to around 90 mph as a starter after hitting the mid-90s in relief. While his dope slider bailed him out in Arizona, two-pitch starters without overpowering velocity tend to make a hash of things in the majors. The ideal situation for the Cardinals is probably Roberts and Alex Reyes in joint long relief roles, taking advantage of their starting history and allowing their velocity to play up in shorter, multi-inning stints.

YEAR	TEAM	LVL	AGE	WHIP	ERA	DRA	WARP	MPH	FB%	WHF	CSP
2018	CRD	RK	22	1.15	6.23	2.47	0.3				
2019	PMB	A+	23	1.74	6.44	8.09	-2.5				
2020	SLN	MLB	24	1.46	5.22	5.28	0.1				

Zack Thompson LHP

Born: 10/28/97 Age: 22 Bats: L Throws: L
Height: 6'2" Weight: 225 Origin: Round 1, 2019 Draft (#19 overall)

YEAR	TEAM	LVL	AGE	W	L	SV	G	GS	IP	H	HR	BB/9	K/9	K	GB%	BABIP
2019	PMB	A+	21	0	0	0	11	0	13^1	16	0	2.7	12.8	19	48%	.455
2020	SLN	MLB	22	2	2	0	33	0	35	35	5	3.8	8.9	35	43%	.305

Comparables: Tony Cingrani, Roman Mendez, Chasen Shreve

You know how sometimes when you're playing a board game, you keep using the same strategy, and it keeps working? You start to wonder if it's just you reading too much into luck, or if everyone else is just missing the obvious move. That's the Cardinals drafting college starters. Thompson slid in the draft due to a 2018 elbow injury and inconsistent command, but a four-pitch arsenal and fastball that tops out in the upper-90s give him at least mid-rotation upside. He was excellent in limited pro innings (he fanned nearly a third of the batters he faced in High-A), and he's likely to move quickly through the Cardinals system. In two years, when he's the number two starter on a Cardinals playoff team headlined by (digs into hat) Justin Williams and Max Schrock, we'll all wonder if the Cardinals cracked the code again, or—whether he's another Marco Gonzales or Michael Wacha or Dakota Hudson—if it's just luck.

YEAR	TEAM	LVL	AGE	WHIP	ERA	DRA	WARP	MPH	FB%	WHF	CSP
2019	PMB	A+	21	1.50	4.05	6.71	-0.3				
2020	SLN	MLB	22	1.42	4.76	4.88	0.2				

St. Louis Cardinals 2020

LINEOUTS

Hitters

HITTER	POS	TEAM	LVL	AGE	PA	R	2B	3B	HR	RBI	BB	K	SB	CS	AVG/OBP/SLG	DRC+	WARP
Conner Capel	OF	MEM	AAA	22	31	5	5	0	2	7	1	6	1	0	.433/.452/.800	145	0.3
	OF	SFD	AA	22	368	39	12	1	9	40	23	84	9	4	.232/.283/.352	76	1.4
Evan Mendoza	3B	SFD	AA	23	223	20	8	1	1	20	14	44	5	1	.248/.293/.311	71	1.0
Delvin Perez	SS	PEO	A	20	506	64	17	3	1	30	27	117	22	9	.269/.329/.325	101	2.1
Max Schrock	INF	MEM	AAA	24	303	42	20	1	2	31	37	49	12	2	.275/.366/.381	103	0.6
Edmundo Sosa	SS	MEM	AAA	23	496	70	18	5	17	62	17	96	2	3	.291/.335/.466	95	2.2
	SS	SLN	MLB	23	10	2	0	0	0	0	1	2	1	0	.250/.400/.250	85	0.0
Lane Thomas	CF	MEM	AAA	23	304	42	17	2	10	44	32	80	11	6	.268/.352/.460	98	1.1
	CF	SLN	MLB	23	44	6	0	1	4	12	4	8	1	1	.316/.409/.684	111	0.5
Ramon Urias	2B	MEM	AAA	25	375	51	24	0	9	52	44	71	4	1	.263/.369/.424	111	1.4
Juan Yepez	1B	PMB	A+	21	115	16	4	0	4	20	10	21	1	0	.275/.351/.431	141	0.7
	1B	SFD	AA	21	59	8	2	0	2	10	5	14	0	0	.231/.288/.385	70	-0.2
	1B	PEO	A	21	101	14	7	0	4	13	11	24	2	1	.284/.366/.500	165	0.9
Wadye Ynfante	OF	PEO	A	21	332	36	7	1	3	19	21	94	12	5	.219/.286/.279	72	1.1
	OF	PMB	A+	21	34	4	0	0	0	0	3	7	0	0	.100/.206/.100	48	0.1

Conner Capel has the speed and arm to hold down any position in the outfield. It's a good thing, too, because his offensive production could play light. There's power there, but plenty of swing-and-miss as well. Think Harrison Bader with the volume turned down. ⓥ **Evan Mendoza** has the bad fortune to be a fringy prospect at the hot corner in a system filled with dynamic third basemen. He hit poorly in Double-A this year while former teammate Tommy Edman tore up the major leagues. In another universe that situation might be reversed, but in this one, Mendoza looks like bench depth. ⓥ **Delvin Perez** has hit only two home runs in nearly 1,100 plate appearances as a professional, and struck out 90 more times than he walked in what was—relatively—a good offensive year. We would note that he went just a few picks after Gavin Lux in the 2016 draft, but that would be mean. ⓥ **Max Schrock** is a high-contact, no-power infielder who would be voted most likely to become the new Stubby Clapp or Bo Hart if you polled fans whose only frame of reference was funnily named Cardinals spare infielders of the early aughts. ⓥ **Edmundo Sosa** combines the slick glove and defensive versatility of a utility infielder with the bat of ... well, with the bat of a utility infielder. We'd say something more clever but we opted to practice the same amount of discipline with this comment that he displays at the plate. ⓥ **Lane Thomas** was one of the fastest players in the major leagues in limited opportunities, so you might say he can flat out fly. Jack Hanna, who attended the same high school as Thomas, would probably reserve that language for a hyacinth macaw rather than a fourth outfielder type. ⓥ **Ramón Urías** held his own in Memphis while developing a little patience at the plate, posting a career-high walk rate. Staple his 2018 power numbers to his 2019 walk rate, and that would be quite the spicy prospect. As is, he's merely a utility infielder in the Yairo Muñoz mold. ⓧ **Juan Yepez** will always be best known—if he's known at all—as the return for fan favorite Matt Adams. He performed well enough in Peoria and Palm Beach to earn a promotion to Double-A, where he predictably struggled. Adams, meanwhile, hit 20-plus homers for a third consecutive season and used Gary Clark Jr. as his walkup music. It's clear who won the trade. ⓧ **Wadye Ynfante** has nearly as many surprisingly placed Y's (two) as he had home runs in 2019 (three). He has the speed to play center field in the majors, but probably not the bat.

Pitchers

PITCHER	TEAM	LVL	AGE	W	L	SV	G	GS	IP	H	HR	BB/9	K/9	K	GB%	WHIP	ERA	DRA	WARP
Tony Cingrani	OKL	AAA	29	1	0	0	7	0	6¹	5	0	5.7	7.1	5	62%	1.42	2.84	4.34	0.1
Austin Gomber	MEM	AAA	25	4	0	0	8	8	45¹	42	5	3.2	10.3	52	43%	1.28	2.98	2.78	1.7
Dominic Leone	MEM	AAA	27	1	0	0	23	0	31²	20	3	4.0	11.9	42	34%	1.07	2.84	2.24	1.2
	SLN	MLB	27	1	0	1	40	0	40²	39	9	4.9	10.2	46	39%	1.50	5.53	5.69	-0.1
Tony Locey	PEO	A	20	1	2	0	10	0	15	15	1	6.0	16.8	28	37%	1.67	6.00	5.21	-0.1
Johan Oviedo	PMB	A+	21	5	0	0	6	5	33²	29	1	3.2	9.4	35	48%	1.22	1.60	4.23	0.3
	SFD	AA	21	7	8	0	23	23	113	120	9	5.1	10.2	128	44%	1.63	5.65	6.32	-1.9
Daniel Ponce de Leon	MEM	AAA	27	8	4	0	16	16	84¹	62	7	4.6	9.2	86	37%	1.25	2.88	2.48	3.4
	SLN	MLB	27	1	2	0	13	8	48²	36	6	4.8	9.6	52	46%	1.27	3.70	3.54	1.1
Zac Rosscup	TOR	MLB	31	0	0	0	2	0	1	3	0	18.0	18.0	2	100%	5.00	27.00	0.00	0.1
	SEA	MLB	31	2	0	0	19	0	14	13	1	9.0	12.9	20	54%	1.93	3.21	3.47	0.3
	LAN	MLB	31	0	0	0	7	0	3	6	1	9.0	12.0	4	60%	3.00	6.00	10.41	-0.2
Alvaro Seijas	PEO	A	20	4	5	0	14	14	80	73	6	3.2	8.0	71	46%	1.26	2.92	5.67	-0.5
	PMB	A+	20	4	1	0	10	10	54¹	54	2	4.3	7.1	43	48%	1.47	2.65	5.98	-0.6
Tyler Webb	MEM	AAA	28	0	1	0	5	0	6²	7	0	2.7	6.8	5	45%	1.35	2.70	4.31	0.1
	SLN	MLB	28	2	1	1	65	0	55	33	7	3.8	7.9	48	43%	1.02	3.76	3.99	0.8
Kodi Whitley	SFD	AA	24	1	4	7	31	0	39¹	31	3	3.0	10.5	46	43%	1.12	1.83	2.80	0.9
	MEM	AAA	24	2	0	2	16	0	23²	21	0	1.5	10.3	27	28%	1.06	1.52	2.21	0.9
Jake Woodford	MEM	AAA	22	9	8	0	26	26	151²	124	22	4.5	7.8	131	37%	1.31	4.15	3.38	4.9

Brett Cecil didn't pitch in 2019. Given how his 2018 went, some Cardinals fans probably hope he won't pitch for the team in 2020, either. ⓧ **Tony Cingrani** didn't pitch in 2019 due to arthroscopic surgery on his throwing shoulder, but that didn't stop the Cardinals from acquiring him as financial ballast in July's Jedd Gyorko trade. If healthy, Cingrani should have no trouble overcoming the new three-batter minimum. ⓧ **Steven Gingery** has a killer changeup—or, he did before he missed the second half of 2018 and most of 2019 rehabbing from Tommy John surgery. This season will mark his first real opportunity to pitch as a professional. ⓧ Biceps and shoulder injuries led to a lost 2019 for **Austin Gomber**, whose combination of okay stuff and excellent command combine to create number three starter upside and journeyman downside. He'll have a place at the end of some roster as long as his health holds up, which is far from a given after this year. ⓧ **Dominic Leone** better hope he has a modified Saberhagen thing going on. He was excellent in '17, bad in '18, and ugly in '19. Maybe he's just a 33 percent shooter? ⓧ **Tony Locey** was a starter at Georgia, but the Cardinals took one look at his stuff (plus curveball, plus fastball) and his command (minus) and plugged him into the bullpen. He missed a ton of bats in limited action in 2019, and will likely rise quickly through the system, as college-age relief arms are wont to do. ⓧ **Johan Oviedo** boasts a mid-90s fastball and absolutely no idea where the ball is going. Tall pitchers often develop late, and he's posted good strikeout numbers even with command issues, but he's nothing more than a bullpen lottery ticket until he can control his delivery better. ⓧ **Daniel Ponce de Leon** would be more interesting if he could find the Fountain of Youth and reduce his age by a handful of years. Instead, he's entering his age-28 season and is probably a bad 20 innings away from falling down the waiver-wire well. ⓧ Just as his first name is missing a letter, **Zac Rosscup** has always had the ability to miss bats. Unfortunately, he also has trouble with missing the strike zone, which is why he played for three teams this year. ⓧ A surprising add to the 40-man roster in advance of the Rule 5 Draft, **Alvaro Seijas** took a step forward in harnessing his fastball that can run up to the mid-90s and his curveball that remains his best out pitch. ⓧ Southpaw **Tyler Webb** doesn't throw hard, impart good spin, or challenge the convention of what makes for a memorable name. He doesn't have job security weighing in his favor, either, since he's a quality LOOGY at a time when one-out appearances are newly outlawed. At least he'll always have 2019? ⓧ **Kodi Whitley** added velocity and spin to his fastball on his way to a dominant season across two levels of the minors. He struck out 28.3 percent of the batters he faced, and tweeted for the first time in nearly a year to thank his minor-league team for the happy birthday wishes. Both tidbits should endear him to Cardinals fans. ⓧ **Jake Woodford** generated a truckload of weak contact on his way to a solid season in the PCL. His stuff screams Edsel, but his command and age give him a chance of getting a test drive in the majors.

Cardinals Prospects

The State of the System

The Cardinals system is below-average on balance, but there are a couple impact bats at the top of the list, and some depth in potential MLB arms.

The Top Ten

1

──── ★ ★ ★ *2020 Top 101 Prospect* **#18** ★ ★ ★ ────

Dylan Carlson   OF   OFP: 70   ETA: 2020
Born: 10/23/98   Age: 21   Bats: B   Throws: L   Height: 6'3"   Weight: 205
Origin: Round 1, 2016 Draft (#33 overall)

The Report: There's breakout prospects and then there's breakout prospects. Carlson is the latter. He had spent the last couple years flashing big tools while putting up fine, but unspectacular performance, albeit while relatively young for his leagues. In 2019 he finally started tapping into his raw power, and a move to center field went well enough—stupid Cardinals Devil Magic—and he's gone from an good org name with some tweener tendencies to a potential five-tool center fielder and national darling. It's not a lock he sticks up-the-middle. Although he's a good baserunner, he's not a true burner. He's filled out in his upper body and has maintained his loose, athletic swing. He has plus bat speed from both sides of the plate and gets to his plus raw power without sacrificing any barrel control. Some .290, 25 HR seasons are likely, and if he can actually handle center in the majors, All-Star games will follow.

Variance: Medium. There's a chance he continues his growth and there's a bit more in the tank at the plate. There's also the risk he's more of a .270, 20 HR corner outfielder that plays center once or twice a week. That's still a very nice major leaguer, but not a star.

Mark Barry's Fantasy Take: While it's not groundbreaking to be enamored with Carlson, I'll go a bit further and say he's one of my five-favorite dynasty prospects, in the land.

2

──── ★ ★ ★ *2020 Top 101 Prospect* **#23** ★ ★ ★ ────

Nolan Gorman   3B   OFP: 60   ETA: 2021/22
Born: 05/10/00   Age: 20   Bats: L   Throws: R   Height: 6'1"   Weight: 210
Origin: Round 1, 2018 Draft (#19 overall)

The Report: The questionable hit tool projection that caused Gorman to slide down draft boards in 2018 crept back into the conversation about his profile this year. The holes in his swing were exposed a bit during his second half stint in the Florida State League with his strikeout rate spiking to over 30%. He's still a teenager and possesses some of the best left-handed power in all of minor league baseball. It's easy power, generated by his raw strength and a quick swing that makes the ball jump off his bat. He also proved to be a capable defender at third this year, showing solid instincts and a strong accurate arm. The Cardinals have aggressively pushed him in his assignments, making him one of the youngest players at each of his stops. That sink-or-swim approach is going to give Gorman the opportunity to make adjustments at the plate and fully tap into his power. If he does, he still profiles as a middle of the order slugging third baseman.

Variance: High. There's the risk that the bat never develops enough to become more than a low average, slugging corner infielder.

Mark Barry's Fantasy Take: The drop in walk rate concerns me more than all of the strikeouts, but Gorman was over three years younger than his High-A counterparts, so growing pains were more or less inevitable. The power is what keeps us coming back, and 30+ dinger seasons are still there to dream on. Bret and Ben had Gorman listed as their 23rd best dynasty prospect in their midseason writeup, and while I might not go that high, it's hard to quibble too much with their expertise.

3. Zack Thompson LHP   OFP: 55   ETA: 2021
Born: 10/28/97   Age: 22   Bats: L   Throws: L   Height: 6'2"   Weight: 225
Origin: Round 1, 2019 Draft (#19 overall)

The Report: Thompson pushed himself into the first round of the draft with a dominant junior year at Kentucky. His frame is right off the "mid-rotation pitching prospect" assembly line— good height, sturdy build. He maintains his low-90s fastball deep into games, and it's a bit of a funky arm action, so the heater sneaks up on you. Both his slider and curve are potentially above-average, and the change is already enough to cross over. He's had multiple arm injuries in the last few years and was used heavily at Kentucky, so while he has the frame to start, we'll have to monitor his durability as he gets stretched out in the pros. I hesitate to call Thompson a safe arm, but health permitting, he has a fairly high floor due to the broad repertoire

Variance: Medium. Thompson has had injury issues in the somewhat recent past, but needs merely refinement in the pros and could move quickly.

Mark Barry's Fantasy Take: I like Thompson about as much you can like an oft-injured, high-usage college arm, which is to say—I like him some. It's cliche at this point in the exercise to say that pitchers are all risky, so I'll spare you here, but I could see Thompson as a SP3 pretty quickly, you know, health permitting.

4   **Ivan Herrera C**   OFP: 55   ETA: 2023
Born: 06/01/00   Age: 20   Bats: R   Throws: R   Height: 6'0"   Weight: 180
Origin: International Free Agent, 2016

The Report: It's just like Ben Franklin said: There are only three certainties in life: Death, taxes, and the Cardinals developing a good catching prospect who will inevitably be blocked by Yadi Molina. In Herrera's case, another aphorism may be appropriate: Timing is everything. The 19-year-old may end up ready for a major-league job right about when Molina is ready to retire—assuming that actually ever happens. Herrera's bat took a step forward last season, as he showed a quick stroke that was short to the ball. Despite the compact swing, he flashes some pullside raw already and the power could play average in games at maturity. Herrera can handle good velocity, but is a bit raw against spin, often out in front. It's nothing too concerning for a teenager seeing full-season arms for the first time, but it's something to keep an eye on going forward.

Herrera moves well behind the plate and has an above-average arm. The receiving should get to at least average as well. There isn't a standout tool here yet, and the bat will need to continue to develop, but a collection of average tools makes you a heckuva prospect when one of them is catcher defense.

Variance: High. Catchers are weird. Teenage catchers are weirder.

Mark Barry's Fantasy Take: Logline: A team of Cardinals back-up catchers and catching prospects team up for a heist to steal Yadier Molina's glove, in a plot to, you know, actually play.

5   **Andrew Knizner C**   OFP: 55   ETA: 2019
Born: 02/03/95   Age: 25   Bats: R   Throws: R   Height: 6'1"   Weight: 200
Origin: Round 7, 2016 Draft (#226 overall)

The Report: Knizner on the other hand, might be stuck behind Yadier Molina for a bit longer. He got a chance midseason when Molina hit the IL for a bit and didn't exactly seize the day. Despite the rough debut, there's good reason to think Knizner will hit going forward. He's short to the ball, and strong enough to drive it to all fields. He's happy to hit the ball where it's pitched, and goes the other way well. Major League spin gave him some trouble, but I'd expect him to make the necessary adjustments to be an above-average hitter overall. He's not generally looking to hit the ball over the fence, but he's strong enough to run into 15ish home runs a year. That's a nice little offensive package for an everyday catcher—assuming there's a job opening soon, I wouldn't exactly be waiting for the Monster.com email.

The defensive side is going to be more problematic and not just by way of comparison to Molina. Knizner is a converted third baseman, and the glove skills are still a bit rough. You could argue the lack of experience just means there's more room for improvement, but while the bat is major-league-ready, Knizner graded out as one of the worst framers in Triple-A and he wasn't any better in the majors. He controls the running game all right despite fringy arm strength, and he's athletic enough you'd like to think he can get the receiving up to acceptable. But there's a ceiling for the glove here, and it's a far cry from the Cards current backstop.

Variance: Low. He's likely to break camp as the backup, I'd expect him to post an above-average offensive line given semi-regular MLB reps, but the glove might limit how many reps the Cardinals want to give him, barring improvements.

Mark Barry's Fantasy Take: If you're looking for a second catcher in an only league or deeper redraft format, Knizner might be a decent bet. For dynasty, value Knizner much like you would have valued Carson Kelly pre-trade. He's a good talent that should hit enough to be one of the 10-15 best catchers in fantasy, if he ever gets a chance to play.

6. Randy Arozarena OF

OFP: 55   ETA: 2019
Born: 02/28/95   Age: 25   Bats: R   Throws: R   Height: 5'11"   Weight: 170
Origin: International Free Agent, 2016

The Report: In 2018, Arozarena bounced between Double-A and Triple-A, mashing at the former, while struggling at the latter. In 2019 he crushed both levels and earned a late-season promotion to St. Louis, finally. He's always had good pop for his size, but the new Triple-A balls were particularly welcoming to his above-average bat speed. Arozarena's swing might be a little bit too line-drive oriented at present to project average game power, but he should create enough hard contact pull side to dump a dozen or so fliners over the left field fence. And sure, I wouldn't be shocked if he's the kind of guy who hits 20 bombs eventually after some "swing tweak," although that's not something you can or should project.

Arozarena has good feel for contact as well, and despite an overly aggressive approach, he doesn't get pull-happy. He won't walk a ton, which is unfortunate given his plus-plus speed, but he should hit .270-.280 generally. Arozarena is a true burner but he's not a true center fielder. I suspect he'd end up average there if he got more reps, but he's a better fit in a corner where he's spent most of his outfield time as a pro. The 2019 performance has mostly disposed of the "tweener" tag, but there's still some risk his approach gets exposed as the league gets more info on him.

Variance: Low. He's probably not quite THIS good, but he has the ability to man all three outfield positions, hit a little bit, run a little bit. Even if he falls short of being an everyday regular, Arozarena is the kind of player that hangs around on major league rosters for the better part of a decade.

Mark Barry's Fantasy Take: Arozarena could do no wrong in 2019, and if you only looked at his three-stop, 2019 sample, you'd probably think he was a top-10ish fantasy guy. He's not, though. And that's not to say he isn't good, or can't be serviceable, but it's more likely that the skillset plays like a fantasy OF4-5 as opposed to a stud.

7. Johan Oviedo   RHP   OFP: 55   ETA: 2021
Born: 03/02/98   Age: 22   Bats: R   Throws: R   Height: 6'6"   Weight: 210
Origin: International Free Agent, 2016

The Report: Oviedo is a massive human, a looming presence on the mound. The fastball sits mid-90s and can touch higher, and with a long stride and high-three-quarters slot, it gets on you quickly and from a steep angle that is difficult to elevate. The command and control are still below-average. He has a fairly short, simple arm action to go with the leg kick and long stride, and can struggle with the timing/syncing the delivery. The secondaries are inconsistent as well. Oviedo tends to slow his arm down on a soft 12-6 curve in the upper-70s. His mid-80s slider is a bit more projectable, although the shape can vary. There's also a firmish change with some tail to it. He'll need to tighten up the mechanics and the offspeed stuff to stick as a starter, and the overall profile is pretty raw for someone with 100+ innings in Double-A, but the frame and arm strength are worth betting on.

Variance: High. It's mostly a fastball at present, and he doesn't consistently throw strikes with...well, anything. It's an ideal frame and the secondaries will flash enough that if he does put it together with more reps, he could blow past this projection. I wouldn't put the mortgage on that bet though.

Mark Barry's Fantasy Take: The fastball is nice, but that's kind of it right now for Oviedo, which super screams reliever to me. Until he gets a little control or adds reliability to the arsenal, I'm not all that interested.

8. Trejyn Fletcher   OF   OFP: 55   ETA: 2024
Born: 04/30/01   Age: 19   Bats: R   Throws: R   Height: 6'2"   Weight: 200
Origin: Round 2, 2019 Draft (#58 overall)

The Report: Fletcher hasn't played a lot of pro ball yet, so there are a lot of things that could happen and a lot of directions this could go in the future. When I saw him near the end of the Appy League season I was struck by a few things. Most obvious was the body. Though he's got a lot of development ahead of him, there isn't much physical projection left and there doesn't need to be. He's very athletic, sturdy and muscular with burst and twitch that show up both sides of the ball. Fletcher has the range and quick first step to handle center, and though I didn't see the arm tested, I've heard great things about that tool as well.

One can easily see where the power will come from after witnessing just one of his incredibly quick and explosive cuts. Unfortunately there is a catch and it is, of course, the hit tool. He actually looked quite lost at the plate and appeared to be lacking in confidence and conviction, constantly caught in between on velocity and flailing at breaking stuff down and away. There's a lot happening mechanically, with some loud hand movement and a big leg kick hindering his ability to stay on time and causing a sort of spiraling effect. Back in September I wrote of Fletcher that he's the type of player whom you can watch strike out three times in four trips to the plate and still walk away fascinated. I believe this will continue to be the case. What does that mean for his career? We'll see.

Variance: Extreme. He's very young and the hit tool is very questionable.

Mark Barry's Fantasy Take: So how do you feel about a mystery box? Inside could be anything—a five-tool stud or a guy that strikes out almost half the time in rookie league en route to a middling and unspectacular minor-league run. Giving up on this sort of profile is obviously silly, but it would take a 300ish-prospect sized league for me to invest.

9 Kodi Whitley   RHP   OFP: 55   ETA: 2020
Born: 02/21/95   Age: 25   Bats: R   Throws: R   Height: 6'4"   Weight: 220
Origin: Round 27, 2017 Draft (#814 overall)

The Report: And here is this year's first true Cardinals Devil Magic entry. Whitley was a Division II arm that didn't even get full pool on Day 3 of the 2017 draft. Now in 2019, he's got among the easier upper-90s velocity you will see. It can look like he's just playing catch with his backstop, and the fastball is a lively enough pitch to be swing-and-miss offering on it's own. Whitley also has the requisite potential plus slider, a mid-80s offering with tilt, and even has a better change-up than you'd expect from your typical late-inning two-pitch power arm. He dominated the minors this year and could be ready to step into the late innings for the Cardinals pen as soon as Opening Day.

Variance: Low. Whitley needs to refine the breaking ball some more to have true late-inning stuff, but the fastball is good enough to keep him employed as a major league reliever for a while.

Mark Barry's Fantasy Take: A career minor-league reliever is likely headed for a decently long major-league career as a, well, you get it. Whitley's role will be determined by his breaker, and his fantasy value will dutifully follow. We should see him this season, but his real value will likely be put to the test in 2021 and beyond, based on how many saves he can wrestle away from whomever dons the closer cap in St. Louis.

10 Elehuris Montero   3B   OFP: 50   ETA: 2021
Born: 08/17/98   Age: 21   Bats: R   Throws: R   Height: 6'3"   Weight: 215
Origin: International Free Agent, 2014

The Report: After a breakout in 2018, the 2019 campaign was more muted for Montero. Wrist injuries limited his time on the field and surely played a role in his poor performance in the Texas League as well. The bat didn't quite pop as much, although he remains fairly quick to the ball. Montero will still show the ability to drive the ball authoritatively to the opposite field, and you'd imagine the above-average raw will still be there when he's fully healthy again. He has begun to fill out a bit more, and is a below-average runner now. His first step and hands at third are all right, and he has plenty of arm, but there's continued risk he will have to move across the diamond if he gets much bigger/less rangy. You're hoping he can battle third base to more or less of a draw, and that the above-average hit/power combination does more than flash in a healthy 2020 season back in the Texas League. That's a lot of ifs, even though Montero is only 21-year-old.

Variance: High. Hey, lost seasons happen. And Montero dealt with wrist injuries and was 20-years-old for almost the entire Double-A season. But the injuries inject more risk into the profile as does the more filled out frame.

Mark Barry's Fantasy Take: Montero's 2019 was a big fat yikes. Sure, a lot of that can be attributed to injuries, but it's hard not to view the Potential Flags as at least orange. There's still a lot to like, offensively, but a David Freese-y upside doesn't really set the fantasy world on fire.

The Next Ten

11 **Mateo Gil SS**
Born: 07/24/00   Age: 19   Bats: R   Throws: R   Height: 6'1"   Weight: 180
Origin: Round 3, 2018 Draft (#95 overall)

The Cardinals 2018 third-round shortstop was known more for his glove as a draft prospect— unsurprising as the son of slick-fielding infielder Benji Gil—but his bat showed some surprising pop in the Appy League last Summer (that was not really part of his father's game). Gil has a prototypical shortstop's build, lean and athletic, with plenty of arm for the 6—he was a half-decent pitching prospect as a prep as well. As a 19-year-old shortstop who wasn't an elite draft prospect, there can be fits and starts on both sides of the ball, and full-season ball in 2020 will ramp up the game speed for him both offensively and defensively, but there's a potential above-average two-way shortstop lurking in the tools profile.

12 **Junior Fernandez RHP**
Born: 03/02/97   Age: 23   Bats: R   Throws: R   Height: 6'1"   Weight: 180
Origin: International Free Agent, 2014

Fernandez shook off two injury-marred seasons and pitched his way into the Cardinals bullpen at the end of 2019. I wouldn't call his upper-90s fastball as easy as Whitley's, but it's plus-plus velocity all the same. He can sink it or cut it a bit down in the zone, although it can flatten out at times up when he's overthrowing. An upper-80s change-up is the best present secondary, and he'll throw it to both righties and lefties. The pitch flashes plus tumble and fade when he successfully pulls the string on it. A slider sits in the same velo band as the change. It's a little less consistent and can get cutterish, although he will show some with power tilt as well. The delivery is high effort and Fernandez may never throw enough strikes where you'll feel comfortable with him closing games, but the stuff is high leverage, and he could end up with two above-average secondaries to go with his 70-grade fastball.

13 Justin Williams   OF
Born: 08/20/95   Age: 24   Bats: L   Throws: R   Height: 6'2"   Weight: 215
Origin: Round 2, 2013 Draft (#52 overall)

We paired Arozarena and Williams on last year's list, and Williams didn't have quite the same upper minors breakout as his outfield mate. He got a late start to 2019 recovering from a fractured hand he suffered in the offseason after punching a TV, and then missed another month over the summer after a promotion to Triple-A. Williams did absolutely rake during his time in Memphis and has always had the potential for plus offensive tools, he's just never put it together for a sustained period of time. The above-average regular ceiling is still there if healthy, and with Ozuna leaving as a free agent, and the subsequent trade of Jose Martinez and Arozarena, there might be a clearer path to a major league role in 2020.

14 Génesis Cabrera   LHP
Born: 10/10/96   Age: 23   Bats: L   Throws: L   Height: 6'2"   Weight: 190
Origin: International Free Agent, 2013

Cabrera remains equal parts prospect and frustrating. He's a lefty with a fastball that regularly hits the upper-90s. It'd be an easy plus-plus offering if the command and control were just a little bit better. He ditched his pretty good slider/cutter thing to focus primarily on his slower—although certainly not slow—12-6 curve in the low-80s. It's potentially pretty good although it's not all the way there yet. He also has a firm change-up in the upper 80s. It has just enough fade and he commands it just well enough on the outer half to righties to make it potentially average. The Cardinals seem to have settled on him as a reliever—which is the right call—and if he tightens up the command (we write this every year) and re-introduces the cutter, he could have late-or-multi-inning utility.

15 Jhon Torres   OF
Born: 03/29/00   Age: 20   Bats: R   Throws: R   Height: 6'4"   Weight: 199
Origin: International Free Agent, 2016

The Cardinals plucked Torres out of Cleveland's complex at the 2018 trade deadline as part of the return for Oscar Mercado. They then jumped him to the Midwest League a month into the 2019 season, and he predictably struggled during his three weeks on the roster. He was overmatched by full-season arms, especially when they threw their offspeed stuff, but a more age appropriate assignment to Johnson City once the Appy League opened went far better.

Torres just looks like a good right field prospect, tall and lean, strong but still projectable. He has plus bat speed and generates good hand/hip separation. He couldn't really lift the ball against Midwest League arms as he was mostly trying to just stay afloat, but the plus raw power got into games more against age-appropriate pitching. He played right field exclusively for Peoria, but they got him the occasional center field rep in Johnson City. That's ambitious, as Torres is a well-below-average runner and takes short strides that limit his range even in right field. There's going to be a ton of pressure on the bat, but there's markers in here that suggest he can make consistent hard contact with more pro experience.

16   Luken Baker   1B
Born: 03/10/97   Age: 23   Bats: R   Throws: R   Height: 6'4"   Weight: 265
Origin: Round 2C, 2018 Draft (#75 overall)

Last year we noted that given Baker's significant defensive limitations—he's a fringy first baseman—"The bat better be great." Admittedly, Palm Beach is an absolutely brutal home park if you are a slugger, but .244 and 10 home runs against Florida State League pitching isn't great, and you could argue is in fact a big flashing red light for a polished college power bat. There weren't huge strikeout issues, as Baker knows what to hack at—although given how long it takes him to uncoil his beer league softball swing, there will be swing-and-miss in the zone—and the plus-plus raw power remains. It's length and strength pop, but Baker is plenty strong—his build is best described as "Scandanavian Wife Carrying Champion." The profile here is pretty all or nothing, and his issues timing High-A arms are more concerning to me than the underlying stat line, but Baker's potential 70 power keeps him on my radar for now.

17   Tony Locey   RHP
Born: 07/29/98   Age: 21   Bats: R   Throws: R   Height: 6'3"   Weight: 239
Origin: Round 3, 2019 Draft (#96 overall)

The Cardinals third-round pick out of Georgia, Locey is a hefty righty with a big fastball. He sits mid-90s with good sink and shows a potentially above-average slider as well. He could struggle with his control both in college and in his pro debut, and his uptempo, full-wind-up delivery can have a lot going on, but he repeats it well enough to project improvements w/r/t throwing strikes. Nonetheless he might be a better fit in the bullpen than the rotation, and only really started full-time his Junior year with the Bulldogs. Locey's curveball shows a pronounced hump in the mid-70s, and his split-change is still inconsistent, so he may not have that pesky third pitch evaluators like to see for starting pitching prospects. He certainly looks the part of an innings eating starter, and I imagine the Cardinals will keep him stretched out for the foreseeable future, but Locey could have the most impact as a power sinker/slider setup man.

18 Jake Woodford   RHP
Born: 10/28/96   Age: 23   Bats: R   Throws: R   Height: 6'4"   Weight: 220
Origin: Round 1, 2015 Draft (#39 overall)

The scouting report on Woodford hasn't really changed much since he was a first round pick in 2015. He features a low-90s heater that can get up to 95 with occasional sink. He'll also show a cut fastball as well. When Woodford is hitting his spots and changing eye levels, he doesn't need much in the way of secondaries, and none of the secondaries are going to jump off the page here anyway. There's a slurvy slider that he works mostly gloveside and off the plate, and a big yakker of a mid-70s curve. He'll use a change-up sparingly as well. None of the offspeed pitches really project as even average, more fringy but useful, as Woodford mixes them in enough to keep hitters off the fastball and cutter. The stuff really hasn't taken as big a step forward as you might have hoped, but given his size and repeatable delivery, Woodford should be able to eat innings in the back of the rotation or the bullpen. He's got a less fastball than Locey, but perhaps a little better shot to start, and he's certainly closer. Pick 'em.

19 Angel Rondon   RHP
Born: 12/01/97   Age: 22   Bats: R   Throws: R   Height: 6'2"   Weight: 185
Origin: International Free Agent, 2016

Like Woodford, Rondon doesn't have big stuff, but mixes everything well enough to project as a potential major league piece. His fastball sits in the low-90s with a bit of armside run, although it can be hittable in the zone. His change-up is potentially above-average. It doesn't always have a ton of fade, but the significant velocity difference—it tops out around 80—can induce swings out of a Bugs Bunny cartoon. Rondon also sells the change well with consistent arm speed. The breaking ball is below-average, a short, slurvy slider either side of 80. If Rondon can tighten up the breaker to give him a gloveside option, he could slot in to the Cardinals pitching staff quickly as a fifth starter or long reliever.

20 Alvaro Seijas   RHP
Born: 10/10/98   Age: 21   Bats: R   Throws: R   Height: 6'1"   Weight: 175
Origin: International Free Agent, 2015

Seijas struggled during his first taste of full-season ball 2018 in Peoria, but a return engagement last year went better and he carried over his success to the Florida State League after a midseason promotion. Seijas is a shorter righty, and the stuff won't wow you, but there's three potentially average pitches in the arsenal. His fastball sits mostly low-90s but can touch 95 and there's some sink and run from his three-quarters slot. Given the arm slot, the low-80s curveball will show surprising depth, and while it's not a huge downer, there's tight, late break, and he commands the pitch well. He also shows a potentially average sinking change, although he can use the curve as an out pitch against lefties as well. Seijas has an uptempo delivery with some effort, and he can have bouts of wildness and command issues due to that. He's also on the slimmer side, so command and durability might force him to the pen despite the well-rounded arsenal.

Personal Cheeseball

PC

Merandy Gonzalez   RHP
Born: 10/09/95   Age: 24   Bats: R   Throws: R   Height: 6'0"   Weight: 216
Origin: International Free Agent, 2013

Merandy Gonzalez's player card tells a very familiar story. He dominated the low minors off of above-average fastball velocity and feel for a below-average, but projectable, curve. He wasn't a non-prospect by any means. He was the kind of OFP 50 with significant relief risk that dots the next ten of lesser systems, but you could picture him sitting 95 in short bursts, and the curve would flash 55 when he got it up into the low-80s. These prospects can hit a wall in Double-A and sure enough Gonzalez struggled as a starter in Jacksonville in 2018. Nevertheless, as he was on the 40-man roster, the Marlins called him up early that year to throw a few innings out of their bullpen because they needed a healthy, fresh arm. As you'd expect, that didn't go any better.

Miami tried to get him through waivers before 2019. He was still prospecty enough that the Giants claimed him and tried to sneak him through themselves, and that's how he ended up with the Cardinals. St. Louis did get him through waivers midseason in the midst of more struggles in Double-A, this time as a reliever. The fastball is low-90s now—and he never got much extension. The curve doesn't look as sharp either, still that below-average one from the low minors. He is—if you want to be technical and a prospect list is inherently littered with weird technicalities—not even part of the Cardinals system at the moment, as he has "elected minor league free agency." Although that might put the agency, so to speak, on the wrong party.

Overall future potential is just that, and it often goes unrealized. I saw a couple Merandy Gonazlez outings back in 2016 when he was in the Penn League with Brooklyn. I saw the possibilities. They weren't lofty, but there was major league utility in his right arm. He didn't end up in the greatest situation for his development, and there were injuries along the way. This story is among the more common in the minor leagues, but definitionally we rarely get to see such denouement within the column inches of a prospect list.

Low Minors Sleeper

LMS

Patrick Romeri   OF
Born: 06/29/01   Age: 19   Bats: R   Throws: R   Height: 6'3"   Weight: 195
Origin: Round 12, 2019 Draft (#365 overall)

The Cardinals paid a little bit overslot to sign Romeri in the 12th round of last year's draft. He was just 17 on draft day and has a plus power/speed combination that could prove worth every penny—with some surplus value to spare. There's ferocious bat speed for a Day 3 prep, but the swing really only has one gear, and there could be a fair bit of swing-and-miss both in and out of the zone. Romeri has a right field profile as well, and while the power, speed, and arm all fit that mold, the hit tool is raw enough to keep him off the list proper for now.

Top Talents 25 and Under (born 4/1/93 or later)

1. Jack Flaherty
2. Dylan Carlson
3. Nolan Gorman
4. Dakota Hudson
5. Zack Thompson
6. Tommy Edman
7. Tyler O'Neill
8. Ivan Herrera
9. Andrew Knizner
10. Jordan Hicks

Carlson has the potential to be a five-tool outfielder who can play center and may have multiple All-Star appearances in his future. The fact that he only ranks second on this list says a whole lot about the type of pitcher Flaherty has turned into. The right-hander just put together a 7.1 WARP season, just missing out on 200 innings and from about the All-Star break through the end of the season, was arguably the most dominant pitcher in baseball. The slider, curve, and sinker are all plus, and he has mid-90s heat that moves. With still another year of eligibility for this list after this year, he's likely to anchor the Cardinals' rotation for the foreseeable future.

The drop-off from Flaherty to Hudson is stark, but while Carlson and Gorman split the two because of the prospect pair's respective ceilings, the other young arm has all the makings of a solid mid-rotation piece. DRA insists his 2019 numbers were a bit lucky, but the sinkerballer avoided the long ball among the best of 'em, and despite pedestrian strikeout numbers, that's a pretty big deal in today's game.

Hudson profiles similarly to Thompson, not so much in terms of stuff or repertoire but in the fact that the latter profiles as a mid-rotation piece once he makes his way to St. Louis. That potential is enough for him to slot in ahead of a trio of major leaguers. Edman is the most surprising name, as the Cardinal Devil Magic Factory got him off the assembly line just in time for him to make a difference down the stretch, whether it was spelling the aging Matt Carpenter at third or the offensively-inept Harrison Bader in center. Edman played five positions for the Cardinals and was worth 2.3 WARP in a little more than a half-season's worth of action. This is probably what he is, but it's pretty danged good.

Edman represents the end of the "polished major leaguer or high-upside prospect" portion of the list. O'Neill is still all potential. It's impressive and powerful potential, to be clear, but until he puts it all together in games he'll still be but a dream. Then there's Hicks, who is an erratic but electric hurler who underwent Tommy John surgery in June 2019. Elite, back-end reliever is still the ceiling there, but we're a ways away from finding out if he can put it all together.

Part 3: Featured Articles

The Baseball Is Juiced (Again)

Robert Arthur

This article originally appeared at Baseball Prospectus on April 5, 2019.

It started when the normally reliable Chris Sale got lit up for three homers by the Mariners in the Red Sox's season opener. It was part of a record number of taters that flew on Opening Day, as starters from Sale to Zack Greinke were taken deep by the handful. Then Christian Yelich hit a home run in each of his first four games, tying yet another MLB record, this one for consecutive games with a dinger to start a season.

It didn't take long for fans and players to begin whispering and tweeting about the baseballs being juiced again. It's early yet for us to come to any definitive conclusion about the 2019 season, but preliminary data shows that the baseball has returned to its aerodynamic peak. Whether that means this season will smash home run records like 2017 did remains to be seen.

Before home run explosion over the last few years, no one worried too much about the baseball's air resistance. While MLB and Rawlings (the company that manufactures the official baseballs) kept track of dozens of metrics to make sure that the ball was consistent from month to month, they didn't measure drag.

But drag is incredibly important in determining how likely a hitter is to knock one out of the park. As baseballs become more aerodynamic, they travel further given a certain initial velocity. A deep fly ball that might have been caught at the warning track can instead go into the first row of the stands. A three percent change in drag coefficient can work to add about five feet to a well-hit fly ball, which can in turn increase home runs league wide by an astounding 10-15 percent.

It's possible to measure the aerodynamics of the baseball using the pitch-tracking radars currently in place in each MLB ballpark. By calculating the loss of speed from when the pitch is released to when it crosses the plate, you can directly measure the drag coefficient on the baseball. I first wrote about the role of decreasing drag in boosting home runs in 2017, and MLB's commission of scientists and statisticians later confirmed that the more aerodynamic baseballs in use that year were largely to blame for the spike in home runs. The same commission rejected some alternate hypotheses, like rising temperatures and a league-wide boost in launch angle pushing more balls over the fence.

The current era has featured some large fluctuations in drag coefficient, leading to first an explosion in 2016 and 2017, and then a dialing back of homers last year. Curious about the record-breaking home run tallies in the last few days, I used the same methodology to measure the aerodynamics of the baseballs so far in 2019.

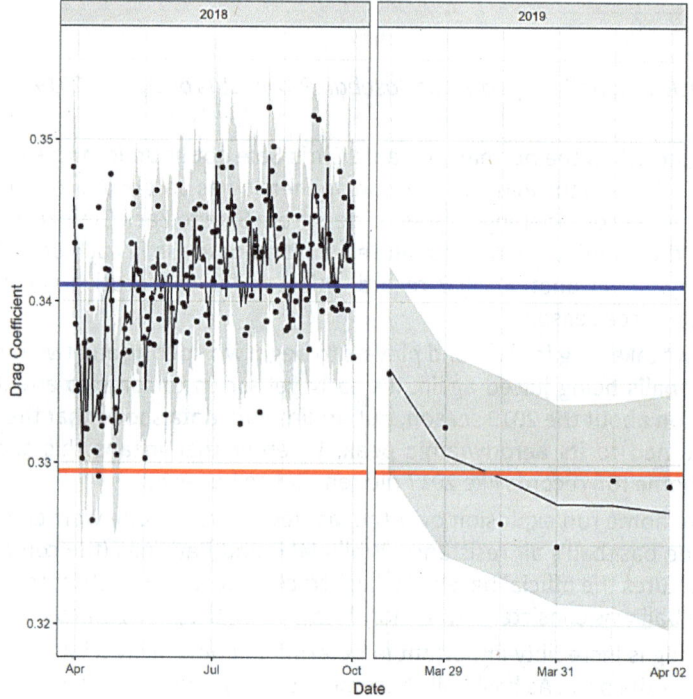

We're only a week into the 2019 season, but the drag numbers so far are among the lowest recorded in the last calendar year. With apologies for gory math, the current 2019 season average drag coefficient (the red line) would be below the 95 percent credible interval (the shaded area) for about nine-tenths of the 2018 season. (I used a Bayesian Random Walk model implemented in INLA to calculate these credible intervals, averaging the drag numbers in each game and adjusting for park.)

There were only a handful of six-day stretches in 2018 that had drag numbers below what we're seeing now, and most were in late June and early July. All of this means that 2019's data so far is quite a bit different than what we saw through most of last year.

These drag coefficients factor out the effects of temperature and air density, so they aren't a product of April cold. However, the numbers could be deceptive if the radars used to track pitches have changed from year to year. I consulted with some experts within baseball who were not aware of any specific modifications to the radar this year that could produce this pattern, but it's an important caveat of which to be aware.

On the one hand, it's only been six days, and we don't quite have the statistical basis to say that these drag coefficients are unprecedented compared to 2018. On the other hand, we've witnessed about 5,000 fastballs so far this season, so it's not as if our sample size is small. At least so far, the baseball has played like it's much more aerodynamic than it was last year. In fact, the current drag coefficient is really only comparable to 2017, when the baseballs were more aerodynamic than they had been in at least a decade.

It's not just fancy radar tracking indicating that the baseball is flying through the air more easily. The current number of home runs per game (as of this writing) is the highest it's been since the heady days of 2017, the year that teams and players broke dinger-related records everywhere you looked. That's especially remarkable considering that we're in what is typically the coldest part of the regular season, when lower temperatures and higher winds tend to suppress offense and keep balls in the air within the park. Comparing only from April to April, this year's rate of home runs per fly ball is even a little bit higher than it was in 2017.

With that said, the current measurements are no guarantee that 2019 will be another year of record-shattering homer hitting. The trouble with the drag measurements is that they are not consistent from June to August, from week to week, or even sometimes from day to day. Whether because of natural manufacturing variation or differences in the underlying supplies of cowhide and thread that go into the baseballs, drag has a tendency to fluctuate up and down over the course of a year. So the homers that fly in the first week of April wouldn't necessarily clear the fence a week later.

It's possible that this one-week drop in drag coefficient subsides and the baseball returns to its 2018 levels. On the other hand, it's almost equally probable that the ball becomes even more slippery and flies ever farther. Either way, it's clear that the baseball's air resistance is something to keep an eye on for the remainder of the 2019 season.

—*Robert Arthur is an author of Baseball Prospectus.*

The Moral Hazard of Playing It Safe

Craig Goldstein

This article originally appeared at Baseball Prospectus on August 6, 2019.

A couple days prior to the trade deadline, amidst a sea of tranquility posing as the lead up to the trade deadline, Bob Nightengale took to Twitter. Nightengale, who was probably wearing his pants backwards at the time, tweeted that MLB GMs were coming around on the idea that the unified trade deadline should be moved back from July 31 to August 15, so they could better assess their positions in the standings and whether they should buy or sell. To which I said:

This might strike some as reductive and churlish. And it might be that, but it isn't really wrong, either. Jeff Quinton wrote a great piece discussing the environmental factors that enable front offices to avoid risk without upsetting the apple cart within their own fanbases. I don't believe that it goes far enough, however. His article gives us the proper framework through which to understand why these behaviors have been allowed to seep into front offices throughout the league. Understanding the reasons behind these actions are different from excusing them, though, and GMs should not be let off the hook for their non-competitive approach to the trade deadline (much less the offseason).

⚾   ⚾   ⚾

It's fair to say that fans as a group have rarely, if ever, been pro-player. It is also fair to say that in the time during and following the Moneyball revolution, the pendulum swung from fans who cared intensely about winning in the moment (and thus might be intolerant of a rebuilding approach) to fans who supported building a team that could compete throughout multiple seasons, viewing the playoffs as a crapshoot, with the thought that getting multiple bites at the apple was a better approach than taking a bigger bite in any one season.

There's nothing wrong with that approach, and I still find merit in that argument. However, it seems that the pendulum has swung too far in that direction. Teams are overvaluing some of the individual factors that make themselves long-term contenders rather than attempting to seize a championship when given the opportunity. It's a difficult needle to thread.

And surely, they (and those in similar positions) would have liked another two weeks to clarify where they stand so as to better marshal their resources. We've all asked for a few more minutes when staring at a menu. But all of these GMs and front office personnel are where they are to make difficult decisions. They have proprietary data and internal analysts dedicated to understanding their position relative to the rest of the league, and how any move in the here and now impacts their long-term vision. To complain (if that report is accurate) that over half the season is not enough to properly assess their season is bullshit of the highest order. Move the deadline, and you'd simply have increasingly discounted trade offers because teams would be acquiring even less control of anyone they're acquiring, rental or not.

Major league front offices are behaving like the managers they lampooned two decades ago. They're effectively sacrificing a runner to second in the ninth inning—not because it's the correct move, but rather because it is safe. It used to be that the phrase "moral hazard" was used to describe general managers who made ill-fated, short-sighted decisions aimed at locking in wins and securing their jobs at the expense of their team's future. Now, general managers are guilty of committing moral hazards in the opposite direction, playing it utterly safe and terrified of becoming scapegoats.

In lieu of bold action, they opt to pussyfoot around a current window of contention, choosing instead to play the long game and stack up years of control like they're blocks in a game of Jenga. GMs pass on signing quality players in free agency because the back-end of the deal might look bad, and because they might be able to squeeze out 70 percent of the production from a player who costs a tenth as much. That's a safer investment, too, because it's also hard to prove a negative—it's impossible to prove that Manny Machado would make the Mets a playoff team in 2019-2020, but it's easy to say that the back half of Robinson Cano's contract sucks. Owners, who rule over GM's jobs, are also humans with human brain processes that will always make the so-called albatross contract uglier than the road not taken.

These days, GMs are remembered for the bad deals they make and the surplus value they generate, not the acquisition of expensive, necessary talents that meet their market worth (or fall slightly short while still providing significant on-field value). And front offices know that one or two expensive misfires can cost them their jobs, no matter how many good deals they make.

No front office exemplifies this ethos more than the Toronto Blue Jays. General Manager Ross Atkins had this to say following the Blue Jays underwhelming trade deadline:

This is by no means the first time that an executive will cite years of control to justify their actions, which is often just another way of saying "don't look at what we got, look at how much we got of it." Atkins touts quantity to elide the discussion of quality—either, that of the players acquired, or those given up. Remember: the other teams presumably value years of control, too.

Atkins also had some thoughts to offer regarding free agents back in early 2018:

The Moral Hazard of Playing It Safe - 113

This ignores, of course, whether the player can create enough value in the front end of a contract to justify the longer term of a deal, and the decline that often occurs in the back end. It also ignores whether the player can fill a need the team requires and put them in a position to compete for and win a championship. But as teams seemingly avoid contention at all, where they might end up having to consider and later justify some of these tough decisions, we still see risk-averse approaches.

Anthony Fenech's article on two trades that recently extended GM Al Avila didn't make got at this issue rather well:

> Passing on those deals was defensible: Both players had yet to break out and trading [Michael] Fulmer—a pitcher who appeared to be a future ace, no matter his injury concerns—would have taken serious gumption, opening Avila up to strong criticism.

Avoiding strong criticism is something each of us can understand as a motivation, but the avoidance of criticism only matters if that criticism is valid. In Fulmer's case, shoving his injury concerns aside affects not only the years that the team controls him (he is currently missing a full season due to Tommy John surgery) but also the quality of those seasons, as his knee and elbow injuries combined to dampen his effectiveness even when healthy enough to pitch. But it was easy to present the then-current image of Fulmer as a top of the rotation pitcher who the team had under its domain for the next five seasons as something to build around. The status quo isn't nearly as often second-guessed as a decision that disrupts it.

⚾ ⚾ ⚾

MLB GMs are risk-averse to a fault. They are ivy-educated and consulting firm-approved, and yet they can't seem to avoid leaving wins on the table in their all-consuming lust for a non-existent $/WAR championship. They are supposed to zig when everyone else zags, and not merely pay lip service to the idea of zigging through a calculated PR plan built on convincing the fan base their approach is novel when it actually apes most of their competitors. Instead they've become far more concerned with making safe, accepted-by-the-new-common-wisdom decisions, such that our prior understanding of what a moral hazard is has become inverted.

I can't blame them entirely, and not only because of the reasons that Quinton illuminated in his article, but also because of the damage wrought by the introduction of the second wild card (WC2) spot. MLB's desire to have more teams in playoff contention has sparked anti-competitive behavior. Teams know now that they do not need to swing big as they assemble their roster because there is a good chance that a mediocre team can either catch fire and capture a division, or muddle along until they back into the WC2.

Simultaneously, the one-game playoff has neutered the WC1, putting an entire season on the flip of a coin like some sort of baseball-obsessed Anton Chigurh. While the one-game playoff makes sense as a way to increase the value of winning a division, it also means that if a front office doesn't like its chances of overcoming a behemoth like the Dodgers or Astros in the offseason, they have few incentives to chase glory. Similarly, the relative inaction in the NL Central at the trade deadline—despite a wide open division—can be explained by the idea that any high-variance investment could still result in only a wild card (or worse) result, given the mere two months left in the season to make an impact.

⚾ ⚾ ⚾

As stated at the top, we should not confuse reasons for excuses. The implementation of the second wild card is just one of many environmental factors that influence how each front office operates. I am convinced that it is one of the larger factors, but I am also convinced that organizations need to shed the yoke of "efficiency at all costs" so that they can instead pursue competition, as the spirit of the game intends. Until they do, we're all deadline losers.

—*Craig Goldstein is an author of Baseball Prospectus.*

Index of Names

Arozarena, Randy 94
Bader, Harrison 18
Baker, Luken 69, 99
Brebbia, John 42
Cabrera, Genesis 44, 98
Capel, Conner 88
Carlson, Dylan 70, 91
Carpenter, Matt 20
Cingrani, Tony 89
DeJong, Paul 22
Edman, Tommy 24
Elledge, Seth 80
Fernandez, Junior 46, 97
Flaherty, Jack 48
Fletcher, Trejyn 71, 95
Fowler, Dexter 26
Gallegos, Giovanny 51
Gant, John 53
Gil, Mateo 97
Goldschmidt, Paul 28
Gomber, Austin 89
Gonzalez, Merandy 101
Gorman, Nolan 72, 91
Helsley, Ryan 55
Herrera, Ivan 73, 93
Hicks, Jordan 57
Hudson, Dakota 59
Jones, Connor 81
Kim, Kwang-Hyun 82
Knizner, Andrew 74, 93
Kruczynski, Evan 83

Leone, Dominic 89
Liberatore, Matthew 84
Locey, Tony 89, 99
Martínez, Carlos 61
Mendoza, Evan 88
Mikolas, Miles 63
Miller, Andrew 65
Miller, Brad 30
Molina, Yadier 32
Montero, Elehuris 75, 96
Muñoz, Yairo 34
Nunez, Malcom 76
O'Neill, Tyler 36
Oviedo, Johan 89, 95
Perez, Delvin 88
Ponce de Leon, Daniel 89
Ravelo, Rangel 77
Reyes, Alex 85
Roberts, Griffin 86
Romeri, Patrick 102
Rondon, Angel 100
Rosscup, Zac 89
Schrock, Max 88
Seijas, Alvaro 89, 100
Sosa, Edmundo 88
Thomas, Lane 88
Thompson, Zack 87, 92
Torres, Jhon 78, 98
Urias, Ramon 88
Wainwright, Adam 67
Webb, Tyler 89

St. Louis Cardinals 2020

Whitley, Kodi 89, 96
Wieters, Matt 38
Williams, Justin 79, 98
Wong, Kolten 40
Woodford, Jake 89, 100
Yepez, Juan 88
Ynfante, Wadye 88